NEW DIRECTIONS FOR CHILD DEVELOPMENT

William Damon, *Brown University*
EDITOR-IN-CHIEF

The Development of Literacy Through Social Interaction

Colette Daiute
Harvard University

EDITOR

Dover Memorial Library
Gardner-Webb University
P.O. Box 836
Boiling Springs, N.C. 28017

Number 61, Fall 1993

JOSSEY-BASS PUBLISHERS
San Francisco

LC
149
.D48
1993

THE DEVELOPMENT OF LITERACY THROUGH SOCIAL INTERACTION
Colette Daiute (ed.)
New Directions for Child Development, no. 61
William Damon, Editor-in-Chief

© 1993 by Jossey-Bass Inc., Publishers. All rights reserved.

No part of this issue may be reproduced in any form—except for a brief quotation (not to exceed 500 words) in a review or professional work—without permission in writing from the publishers.

Microfilm copies of issues and articles are available in 16mm and 35mm, as well as microfiche in 105mm, through University Microfilms Inc., 300 North Zeeb Road, Ann Arbor, Michigan 48106-1346.

LC 85-644581   ISSN 0195-2269   ISBN 1-55542-720-0

NEW DIRECTIONS FOR CHILD DEVELOPMENT is part of The Jossey-Bass Education Series and is published quarterly by Jossey-Bass Inc., Publishers, 350 Sansome Street, San Francisco, California 94104-1310 (publication number USPS 494-090). Second-class postage paid at San Francisco, California, and at additional mailing offices. POSTMASTER: Send address changes to Jossey-Bass Inc., Publishers, 350 Sansome Street, San Francisco, California 94104-1310.

EDITORIAL CORRESPONDENCE should be sent to the Editor-in-Chief, William Damon, Department of Education, Box 1938, Brown University, Providence, Rhode Island 02912.

Cover photograph by Wernher Krutein/PHOTOVAULT © 1990.

Epigraph in Chapter Two reprinted by permission of the publishers from *Mind in Society: The Development of Higher Psychological Processes* by L. S. Vygotsky, Cambridge, Mass.: Harvard University Press, Copyright © 1978 by the President and Fellows of Harvard College.

Manufactured in the United States of America. Nearly all Jossey-Bass books, jackets, and periodicals are printed on recycled paper that contains at least 50 percent recycled waste, including 10 percent postconsumer waste. Many of our materials are also printed with vegetable-based ink; during the printing process these inks emit fewer volatile organic compounds (VOCs) than petroleum-based inks. VOCs contribute to the formation of smog.

Contents

EDITOR'S NOTES   1
Colette Daiute

PART ONE: CONTEXTS FOR LITERACY

1. Families as Social Contexts for Literacy Development   11
Catherine E. Snow
Parents' conversations with children provide a foundation for literacy when
they engage children in talk about past events, explaining complex processes
and defining words, and in other "literate" speech.

2. A Sociocultural Perspective on Symbolic Development   25
in Primary Grade Classrooms
Anne Haas Dyson
Children's interactions in social worlds influence the content, structure, and
context of literacy.

3. Young Authors' Interactions with Peers and a Teacher: 41
Toward a Developmentally Sensitive Sociocultural Literacy Theory
Colette Daiute, Carolyn H. Campbell, Terri M. Griffin,
Maureen Reddy, Terrence Tivnan
Social interaction among peers during literacy tasks in school reveals that
intense focus on text in the context of social and affective interaction
supports literacy development.

PART TWO: LITERACY SKILLS IN CONTEXT

4. Learning Vocabulary in Preschool: Social and Discourse   67
Contexts Affecting Vocabulary Growth
David K. Dickinson, Linda Cote, Miriam W. Smith
Teachers can support children's reading development by talking with them
in linguistically challenging ways, especially by using rare words.

5. The Social Construction of Spelling   79
Maureen Reddy, Colette Daiute
Children's concern about how to spell words when they write is part of the
broader social picture of literacy and integrally related to other facets of
literacy development.

6. The Social Construction of Written Narratives   97
Colette Daiute, Terri M. Griffin
Children use writing to make sense of academic material and events in school and in their lives, thus interpreting knowledge and experience through their narrative writing rather than merely mastering written language as a communication skill.

7. Synthesis   121
Colette Daiute
The chapters in this volume articulate several principles that can guide literacy research and practice.

INDEX   125

EDITOR'S NOTES

This volume, *The Development of Literacy Through Social Interaction,* is about literacy as a social process. For many years, reading and writing were defined in terms of the structure of texts, and children's reading and writing performance was described with reference to their abilities to manipulate the units of written language, including letters, words, sentences, and paragraphs. Since the 1980s, researchers and educators have emphasized cognitive processes involved in composing and comprehending, as defined mostly by the strategies used by skilled adult readers and writers. It has recently become clear, however, that the social context of literacy plays a major role in the development of children's oral and written language. This shift to social context involves new ways of approaching the study of literacy problems. Rather than looking for deficits within the child, social theories account for how children negotiate written language based on the values, resources, and practices of the diverse contexts in which they live. In presenting research designed around the theme of the interdisciplinary study of literacy development, we focus here on social interaction as the core of a new understanding about what it means to become literate.

This understanding that children develop reading and writing in social contexts is helpful in addressing a variety of issues. Social understandings of literacy development are useful in gaining insights about the nature of discourse that children from different backgrounds bring to school. Some types of interaction in the home, for example, may privilege children for success in school-based literacy. Several chapters in this volume address such issues directly. In addition, if literacy is, at least in part, a communication process, then the nature of communication about written language relates to children's development of literacy strategies. Finally, as we realize that the traditional categories for analyzing oral and written language do not explain either development or practice, we need more powerful and integrated perspectives. The nature of children's participation in social discourse is likely to have an impact on their intellectual capacities.

Researchers have begun to examine connections between family discourse patterns, children's spontaneous oral language, interactions with friends, and the written language tasks that they encounter in school. Emphasis on the nature of discourse required to prepare children for school-based literacy has also underscored the need to understand relationships between literacy instruction and the functions of literacy as children perceive them. Thus, the effort to account for literacy problems in terms of contextual issues rather than presumed deficits in the child has broadened inquiries into literacy and, in some cases, literacy instruction. Writing projects that might make a difference in the community are more salient and enjoyable to children than are worksheet tasks, but there is still a lot to learn about the nature of socially mediated literacy.

The purpose of this volume is to examine a range of inquiries on the social nature of literacy development in a variety of contexts among children of about three through twelve years of age. We consider literacy in the home and at school, interactions between parents and children, between teachers and children, and among classmates. Likewise, we consider a range of literacy skills, expanding beyond traditional notions to new understandings of what it means to become literate. Moreover, we discuss skills that have only recently been associated with the process of becoming literate, including oral language, storytelling styles, and social interaction strategies. We also present new ways of thinking about traditionally noted skills such as spelling and vocabulary.

Other similarities of the research projects described here include their grounding in interdisciplinary perspectives on literacy and the exploration of literacy in the context of child development. We link social factors to cognitive and linguistic factors. Some of us are working to integrate understandings about cultural and affective factors. The research thus explores complex theories of literacy and begins to identify processes that lead to change in children's reading and writing skills.

Two notions of interaction underlie much of the research in this volume, and the inherent tensions between these notions motivate some of the questions addressed in the studies discussed here. Based on the theory of L. S. Vygotsky, social interactionist theories of literacy development assume that written language takes on meaning for children in the context of culturally relevant social situations. Vygotsky (1978) argued that all thought occurs first in social interaction—defining the interpsychological nature of thought as a social phenomenon—and only gradually becoming internal or intrapsychological. Bakhtin (1981) extended this notion of social thought turning inward by proposing the concept of genres. Speech genres reflecting the different voices a person hears in the myriad cultural and social spheres of his or her life create the foundation for individual thought and discourse. While many researchers and educators believe in the importance of such social reproduction, researchers differ in how they relate it to an individual child's literacy. Some posit that all thought is social (Gee, 1991), which diminishes the need to account for individual differences, and others focus on relationships between social, developmental, and personal factors, as the contributors do in this volume.

Piagetian theory emphasizes a different type of interaction: the child's interaction with the environment. According to Piaget (1967), the child's mind is structured in such a way that he or she can construct theories about the world based on his or her interactions with people and phenomena in the world. The related cognitive developmental theory of literacy describes the child as constructing the rules of written language (as he or she did for oral language) (Ferriero and Teberosky, 1979). While many researchers work within the social interactionist and environmental interactionist proposals, we explore the tensions and possible connections between them. Many researchers and educators have found the influence of social interaction to be appealing, but the nature and necessity of social interaction for literacy and learning are still not clearly defined. Many questions remain: In what ways does social interaction support literacy and learning? In what ways do specific types of social interaction relate to cognition and cognitive development? The chapters in this volume address these and other questions as they play out the general proposals about the role of social interaction in literacy advanced by scholars such as Vygotsky and Bakhtin.

The projects described here differ in terms of their definitions of literacy and literacy development and in terms of their goals. For example, in Chapter One, Catherine E. Snow defines the end point of literacy as the reading and writing of a skilled college student. In Chapter Two, Anne Haas Dyson defines literacy as a cultural tool for taking action in the world. In Chapter Three, Colette Daiute, Carolyn H. Campbell, Terri M. Griffin, Maureen Reddy, and Terrence Tivnan define literacy in terms of its intellectual, affective, and social functions, thus focusing on written language as a tool for learning, reflecting, and acting in a community. The different emphases in these definitions reflect the goals of the literacy research projects. Snow and, in Chapter Four, David K. Dickinson, Linda Cote, and Miriam W. Smith discuss a range of language and literacy measures collected over a number of years, including standardized achievement scores, which they use to relate processes to outcomes in terms of measures of mainstream culture. Dyson considers children's written language as it evolves in the context of social relationships among a small group of children interacting at journal-writing time in school over several years. Daiute and her colleagues are investigating children's perspectives on literacy, based on the hypothesis that literacy instruction is missing the mark, at least in part, because it ignores how children express themselves and how they approach problems in their everyday lives. These diverse perspectives all suggest a revision of traditional definitions of what it means to become literate.

Organization of This Volume

While all of the chapters in this volume consider different contexts of literacy development and revised notions of literacy skills, the chapters are organized into two sections on the basis of major focus. The chapters in the first part of the book are organized around theory about the role of social interaction in the context of important relationships in children's lives. Relationships with family, teachers, and friends have increasingly been seen as contexts for literacy and learning. As we consider family and friends part of education, issues of affect make their way into what was previously seen as purely a cognitive and linguistic domain. Similarly, as teachers become collaborators in education as well as transmitters of information, the cognitive and individualistic emphases of schools broaden. By examining how diverse contexts contribute in different ways to children's literacy, we get a fuller picture of literacy in children's lives.

Drawing on a longitudinal study of literacy development in a relatively large number of children in home and school contexts, Snow identifies family discourse patterns as they relate to literacy development. Proposing the useful notion of "problem space," Snow characterizes the parents' role as one of providing the right types of conversational challenges to children when they are ready to address them and integrate them into their discourse. Children who succeed with literacy are those whose parents engaged them in conversations about past events, about processes requiring explanation, and about language (for example, word definitions). Thus, Snow's research highlights how children benefit when their parents socialize them into literate ways of talking, since such modes of discourse are the basis of school and test discourse.

Dyson reviews several ethnographic studies of children's writing development in the primary grades. She examines literacy development from within children's social worlds, and she illustrates the sociocultural dynamics through which children negotiate a functional role for writing within their symbolic repertoires. In contrast to Snow's research, Dyson focuses on the contexts and purposes of particular uses of language as they evolve in social interaction among children. She shows how actions surrounding language, rather than language use per se, influenced the course of several children's progress as writers over time.

Daiute, Campbell, Griffin, Reddy, and Tivnan focus on research that compares and contrasts the processes and outcomes of collaborative composing sessions of teacher-student and peer dyads. The chapter outlines theoretical issues of explicit teaching and peer collaboration as they relate to reading and writing development in the classroom context. Data from a study of writing by children working alone, with peers, and with their teacher serve as the basis for the thesis that since reading and writing are extensions of oral language, they must be explored as developmental processes as well as social constructs influenced by enculturation and instruction. Research results provide a framework for comparing and contrasting the explanatory power of Vygotskian and Piagetian theories with regard to the development of writing skills. Teachers and other experts can instruct children on literacy features that are valued in school, but children must take control over their own literary voices and purposes to benefit from an expert writer's instruction and to develop their own composing strategies.

The three chapters in the second part of this volume redefine so-called basic skills in the context of social theories of literacy. Dickinson, Cote, and Smith focus on the cognitive nature of classroom talk and its impact on vocabulary development. They offer a theoretical discussion on the nature of decontextualized literacy skills and their relationship to conversations in preschool classrooms and to reading achievement. Making the link between talk and vocabulary, these authors identify different cognitive functions underlying talk by teachers and children in preschool and primary grade classrooms. Their analyses isolate relationships between certain types of talk and vocabulary development, an important predictor of reading success.

In Chapter Five, Reddy and Daiute discuss spelling, which is often considered the most basic of literacy skills. They argue that spelling skills continue to be a concern of children well into the elementary grades, as these skills relate to other aspects of literacy, including social context, knowledge domains, and children's theory building about written language. Moreover, children's focus on spelling in the context of other rhetorical aspects of writing challenges two commonly held assumptions about spelling: the assumption that correct spelling is a prerequisite to writing and the theoretically distinct assumption that spelling distracts from social and conceptual aspects of literacy.

In Chapter Six, Daiute and Griffin focus on children's written narratives—in particular, children's use of written narratives to make sense of academic material and events in school and in their lives. This perspective differs from the more typical approach of examining children's literacy as a set of skills in its focus on meaning rather than structure, the aspect of narrative most often considered in school curricula. Their study of children's written narratives extends research on the development of oral narratives that has shown how children use linguistic devices to express their interpretations of and feelings about poignant events in their lives. By contrasting narrative texts and composing sessions by teacher-student and peer pairs, Daiute and Griffin have gained information about different ways of constructing written narratives in classrooms. They set their study in the context of the broader debate about the nature of narrative, drawing implications for future research and practice.

Issues

Diverse perspectives on several important issues, including relationships between oral and written language, contextualized and decontextualized skills, and methodologies, emerge across the chapters.

Different Perspectives on Social Interaction. Three different perspectives on social interaction weave through the chapters in this book. For Dyson, literacy is social interaction. She examines the development of children's written symbolizations as they occur in the social context of the classroom. Through her examples and discussion of the symbols, meanings, and approaches to literacy that occur in the classroom context, Dyson illustrates the truly embedded nature of written language. For Dyson, literacy development is based not on the accrual of skills but rather on the engagement of children with others through the act of writing. In contrast, Snow and Dickinson, Cote, and Smith examine connections between oral and written language as different components of literacy. These scholars address cultural issues that underlie literacy by examining a broad range of language and literacy measures and identifying connections between private conversations in families, conversations in the classroom, and children's scores on a nationally normed reading test. To gain insights about relationships between instruction and development, Daiute, Campbell, Griffin, Reddy, and Tivnan examine social interaction in two ways. First, social interaction is a window on children's internal processes, providing links between social and individual aspects of literacy. Second, supported by social interaction, children recreate the written language models of their cultures through intense examination of texts.

Oral and Written Language. The chapters in this book examine in different ways the relationships between oral and written language. All assume important relationships between oral and written language, but the role of oral language as a context differs. Dyson focuses on the social functions of oral language as the context, impetus, and content of the writing and symbols children create in the primary grades. Snow and Dickinson, Cote, and Smith focus on how decontextualized skills like defining words and talking about past events are central to children's ability to process written language in ways required in school and measured on tests. Daiute and her colleagues consider children's spontaneous oral language during social interactions around literacy tasks as essential supports for their analytical work with text. Thus, Snow, Dickinson, Cote, and Smith, and Daiute and her colleagues focus on boundaries between oral and written language to understand how each differs from and supports the other, whereas Dyson treats oral and written language as a unit of analysis. Another contrast is that Daiute and her colleagues find that children's familiar, albeit immature, oral language strategies support their work with text, whereas Snow finds that children need to be engaged in talk that is different from their spontaneous discourse. Together, these perspectives indicate that written language must be examined in relation to oral language not only to gather evidence of linguistic capacities, as has been done in the past, but also to understand children's reading and writing within the broader context of how they use language to express and reflect on their experience and ideas. These diverse perspectives on oral and written language indicate the complexity of literacy and the need for more research.

Research Perspectives. The chapters in this book are grounded in several disciplines. The work by Snow and by Dickinson, Cote, and Smith is grounded in child language research. They consider written language as an extension of a child's first language; thus, they integrate social issues with developmental factors. Dyson's ethnographic perspective considers social units and the development of literacy within social and cultural frameworks. Daiute and her colleagues bring the perspectives of developmental psychology and instruction to issues of social interaction.

Methodology. The three perspectives on social interaction presented in this book are defined in part by the modes of inquiry chosen by the researchers. By using ethnography over several years in one classroom, Dyson has gained insights into the cultural mores of the children studied, the classroom culture, and the individual children's personalities. The contextual details of her ethnographic inquiry provide information on how children infuse symbols with meanings and the ways in which such symbols reflect diverse meanings depending on the particular contexts of use.

The multiple types of discourse analyses in the research of Daiute and her colleagues serve to link social interaction contexts with changes in children's texts over time, thus linking the broader culture represented by the teacher to the youth culture represented by the children's interactions. These detailed analyses of talk and text provide information about how different types of talk and approaches to school tasks relate to children's representations of text. The exploration of statistical relationships across several years and a broad range of variables allows Snow and Dickinson, Cote, and Smith to relate different types of language use to school-based literacy outcomes.

In summary, the picture of literacy created in this volume is a collage. The central theme of social interaction in literacy development is covered through diverse snapshots of different styles. This collage lays out theoretical bases, research questions, and findings that together suggest emerging themes for the redefinition and future exploration of literacy.

The contributors and I are indebted to Tamara Wilkerson. Her help in editing, creating tables, and pulling this volume together in other ways was invaluable.

References

Bakhtin, M. M. "Discourse in the Novel." In *The Dialogic Imagination: Four Essays by M. Bakhtin.* (C. Emerson and M. Holquist, trans.) Austin: University of Texas Press, 1981.

Ferriero, E., and Teberosky, A. *Literacy Before Schooling.* Portsmouth, N.H.: Heinemann Educational Books, 1979.

Gee, J. *What Is Literacy?* Brookline, Mass.: The Literacies Institute, 1991.

Piaget, J. *Six Psychological Studies.* New York: Random House, 1967.

Vygotsky, L. S. *Mind in Society: The Development of Higher Psychological Processes.* (M. Cole, V. John-Steiner, S. Scribner, and E. Souberman, eds.) Cambridge, Mass.: Harvard University Press, 1978.

Colette Daiute
Editor

COLETTE DAIUTE is associate professor at the Graduate School of Education, Harvard University.

PART ONE

Contexts for Literacy

Parents' most important contributions to their children's literacy development may come through language interactions rather than print-related activities.

Families as Social Contexts for Literacy Development

Catherine E. Snow

This chapter presents an overview of a number of ways in which social interactions within the family support literacy acquisition. There has, of course, been a substantial amount of research devoted to this topic, much of it starting from the observation that middle-class and highly educated families typically produce more successful school learners than do working-class families. A major site for looking at family interactions has been book reading, on the assumption that early exposure to literacy promotes later literacy skills. The research I discuss here differs from previous efforts in two major ways. I have not engaged in social class comparisons, preferring to compare within relatively high-risk samples the families who successfully support their children's literacy development to those who do not. And I have focused less on literacy-specific interactions than on language interaction in general as a source of skills that are relevant to literacy.

The findings reported here derive from three major studies in which I have been involved: a study of the correlates of school literacy among children from low-income families attending second through seventh grades (Snow and others, 1991), a study of children in U.S. schools who come from

The research discussed in this paper has been supported by the National Institutes of Education (*Unfulfilled Expectations*), the Spencer Foundation (the United Nations International School Study and current support for the Home-School Study of Language and Literacy Development), the Office of Educational Research and Improvement (the New Haven study), and the Ford Foundation (initial stages of the home-school study). I thank my several collaborators on those studies, in particular, Herlinda Cancino, Patricia Velasco, Patton Tabors, and David Dickinson.

families where a language other than English is spoken (Snow, 1991a), and an ongoing longitudinal study of language and literacy development in children from low-income families, from age three through fourth grade (Snow, 1991b). In all of these studies, a major question was, Which activities or interactions in the home contribute to children's school achievement, particularly as related to literacy?

Before presenting findings from these studies, though, it is important to define the outcomes of interest. We have data on traditional literacy outcomes, for example, standardized tests of reading and writing samples, but we have also collected data on domains that we consider prerequisite to or closely correlated with traditional literacy—in particular, certain aspects of oral language. In order to clarify how our findings about oral language skills relate to literacy, it is necessary to outline the model of literacy development that has undergirded these various studies. After presentation of that model, I turn to summaries of relevant findings from the three studies. The basic point of the discussion is that parents' most important contributions to their children's literacy development may come through language interactions rather than print-related activities.

A Model of Literacy Development

Foremost, assessment of family influences on the development of literacy requires a decision about what we mean by *literacy*. What developments or accomplishments in childhood should be considered relevant to literacy development? The model of literacy that has guided my investigations (see Snow, in press; Snow and Dickinson, 1991, for expanded presentations; see also Dickinson, Cote, and Smith, this volume, for a similar view) views sophisticated, college-level literacy as representing the culmination of several strands of development, some of which start well before anything like formal reading or writing occurs. College-level reading, for example, involves the ability to read in ways adjusted to one's purpose (to enjoy light fiction, to memorize factual material, to analyze literature), to learn facts and discover ideas in texts, to judge the writer's point of view, and to incorporate information and perspectives from text into one's own thinking but also to question and disagree with information and opinions expressed.

The abilities that emerge within these various strands represent *problem spaces,* that is, domains that children have to work on or receive instruction in. Use of the term *problem space* is meant to emphasize learners' active roles in reorganizing their own knowledge, after recognizing discrepancies between their current theory or notion and some information in the world. Some problem spaces, such as figuring out irregular past tenses in English, are fairly common for children at a particular developmental level; others, such as figuring out the circle of fifths in music or endgame strategies for chess, emerge at a particular stage in the mastery of a domain rather than at some point defined by age or cognitive stage. A crucial characteristic of problem spaces, though, is that the current problem attracts considerable cognitive energy from the child, and can be worked through more quickly if relevant informative and helpful interactions with adults are available.

Familiar Reading Skills. Let me illustrate this model by discussing a skill traditionally associated with reading readiness—*letter recognition.* Clearly, before one can begin to read words in an alphabetic language, one must be able to differentiate letter shapes and associate each letter with its proper sound or sound family. Many children struggle with the problem of letter recognition during the preschool period, fitting magnetic letters into puzzle forms, perhaps learning to print their own names and other important words, and seeking out familiar letters on signs or in books. Most children work hard and encounter frustration at this stage of development, confusing *b* and *d* for a period of time, or forgetting how certain letters are written. In some families, they receive help, support, and considerable positive recognition even for somewhat primitive efforts at writing with invented spellings, copying words, or identifying letters during this stage. At some point, letter recognition is smooth, reliable, and ultimately automatized such that it does not require much cognitive energy. In fact, letter recognition becomes so skilled that older children and adults can read relatively degraded print without difficulty. Letter recognition is no longer a problem space.

Letter recognition is a crucial skill in literacy, though well defined and quite limited in scope. Also well defined but somewhat more complex is the skill of *phoneme segmentation*—figuring out the compositional units of words and matching the sounds with the letters (the basic alphabetic principle). Phoneme segmentation by first graders has been widely found to be a good predictor of reading progress (for example, Juel, 1988; Stanovitch, 1986). Phoneme segmentation and phoneme-grapheme mapping in particular involve more complexity than letter recognition in languages, such as English, where the spelling rules are abstract and morphological rather than concrete and phonemic. Children's entry into the problem space of phoneme segmentation is indicated by their interest in rhymes and other forms of sound play; pig latin and other such segmentation-based invented languages emerge only after children have achieved a fairly high degree of automatization with segmentation.

Obviously, though, reading involves more than letters and segments. The development of the literacy skill called *word recognition* relies on the achievement of relatively late stages of skill in letter recognition and phoneme-grapheme mapping, with the additional problems of blending sounds into words, figuring out syllable stress and thus the pronunciation of vowels in multisyllabic words, and connecting the sounded-out word with a meaning. The process of acquiring word recognition skill typically starts with formal reading instruction in kindergarten or first grade and continues for novel and complex words into the late elementary years. As for the other skills discussed, word recognition is effectively acquired only when it is automatized to the point that little cognitive energy goes into the process. Normal reading with comprehension relies on the fast and automatic recognition of most of the words in the text, and reading with comprehension is slowed and disrupted if effort must be expended on individual words in the text.

Automatized reading comprehension is a function of practice with the target words, not just of having automatized the component processes of letter recognition and phoneme-grapheme mapping. This is made clear by the difficulties that skilled readers encounter when reading in a second language, for example, or even when reading in English with modified spelling. In his novel *Riddley Walker,* Russell Hoban (1982) writes of life around Canterbury (Cambry) in a postdoomsday English that differs from twentieth-century English mostly in its spelling rules, though the occasional use of wonderfully evocative innovated word forms and the reliance on grammar more typical of oral than written language also challenge the reader:

> Looking up in to the black where the goast of Power circelt blyn and oansome like a Drop John round the lost hump of Cambry I larft I yelt, "SPIRIT OF GOD ROAD WITH ME!"
>
> Dark of the Moon it wer. Pas the failing moon of my getting and fulling on tords the moon of my bearthing I gone to the hart of the wud I gone to the stoan wood in the hart of the stoan I gone to the woom of her what has her woom in Cambry.
>
> The black sky dint change colour nor the stoans dint go wite nor the dogs dint runny on ther hynt legs with the shyning colours coming thru them it just stayd solid black. No lerting from the dogs so I lit a candl. Up jumpt the shadders and shaking on the walls and rubbl. In amongst them stoan trees there wer what you myt call a notness of some 1. Some 1 ben roun there nor not too long befor me. No 1 was there now tho. Lookit in the hidey hoal where Greanvine livet. Emty.
>
> Lookit in the out poast. HOAP OF A TREE stil on the wall and the picter of Goodparley with the vines and leaves growing out of his mouf. No 1 there [pp. 191–192].

Note that the majority of words in this passage, as in the whole book, are standard English spellings; nonetheless, the unfamiliarity even without any particular lexical or mapping complexity of *stoan* for stone, *myt* for might, *wud* for would, *poast* for post, and so on disrupts reading enormously, perhaps more for skilled readers than for those who are not yet able to rely on automatized word recognition.

Finally, of course, traditional sketches of reading include as a separate component reading comprehension, the ability to extract or formulate meaning from text. Reading comprehension is obviously even more complex and multiply determined than word recognition, and it is not a skill that ever becomes fully automatized for all text types. While most adults with a high school education can read a newspaper or sports magazine without consciously working to comprehend, even those of us with advanced degrees struggle to understand physics textbooks, instructions for filling out tax forms, and transcripts of presidential news conferences. Some comprehension strategies that are taught to young children explicitly inhibit automatization of comprehension; these include metacognitive strategies such as "stop at the end of every paragraph and ask yourself what it was about" or "preview the section headings and try to predict what the passage is going to tell you." Thus, I treat reading comprehension here not as a component strand of literacy development but as the much more amorphous product of many component skills.

Oral Language Skills Prerequisite to Reading. The three processes discussed so far—letter recognition, phoneme segmentation and mapping, and word recognition—are well recognized within the field of reading as prerequisite or component reading skills, and family interactions can of course support the development of any of these. But other skills in the domain of oral language use are just as critical to efficient and effective reading, and these are even more likely to be developed in the context of family interactions. These include oral language skills such as familiarity with relatively rare vocabulary, understanding the lexical and grammatical strategies for adjusting to a nonpresent audience, identifying the perspective of the listener so as to provide sufficient background information, knowing the genre-specific rules for various forms of talk such as narrative and explanation, and so on.

Vocabulary has been associated with literacy development across a variety of studies, for children speaking different languages and learning to read in a variety of instructional settings (Anderson and Freebody, 1981; see Dickinson, Cote, and Smith, this volume, for a review). Some of the mechanisms by which a larger vocabulary promotes reading are obvious; in a language such as English, where pronunciation of many words is not easily predictable from their spelling, access to stored target forms helps eliminate mispronunciations and misidentifications in most cases. Vocabulary also predicts literacy, though, in languages such as Spanish, where the spelled form is absolutely unambiguous as to pronunciation. It seems likely, then, that vocabulary knowledge in these cases indexes world knowledge—background information that the reader can use to help in the task of comprehension.

Beyond vocabulary, though, performance on tasks like describing pictures or telling stories in a way that is relatively complete, detailed, and comprehensible relates to reading. Why do we find this connection? The ability to give a good, complete picture description requires analysis of what it is the listener (who, of course, cannot see the picture) needs to know in order to understand what the picture is about. Furthermore, compressing the needed information into a comprehensible oral language format requires the use of complex grammar (relative clauses, appositions, subordination) as well as effective self-monitoring. Consider the following examples of picture descriptions from fifth graders who were native speakers of Spanish. The first comes from Elena, a girl reading above grade level:[1]

1   There's some baseball players.
2   And they're playing.
3   And a girl went to hit the ball.
4   And then she's going to hit it but it's too close.
5   So she can't hit it.
6   And there are two boys that are talking.
7   And they going to play too.
8   And there's a catcher.
9   And there's another boy that throws the ball.
10 Is the pitcher . . .
11 And there's there's numbers in the floor.
12 And there's a cap # there's a cap behind the girl
13 So if the ball goes away it won't go away because the cap holds it.
14 And here are two boys talking about baseball players
15 or maybe about something else.
16 And there's a boy there with a bat on their hands.
17 And they . . . there's another boy there that has (a) . . .
18 a glove to catch the ball in the other game.

The next description, of the same picture, comes from Carmen, who was reading below grade level:

1   There's three boy . . .
2   One got # they're playing baseball . . .
3   The girl has hair ye // yellow hair . . .
4   It got walls.
5   The boy has the hair up.
6   The girl gonna hit the ball.
7   The other girls // she's talking with a boy . . .
8   The girl has a dress.
9   It's red and white.
10 She got the eye black.
11 Her face is like red.
12 It got black and red.
13 The boy got the shirt white and the pant white.
14 The boy has another bat.
15 He got his hair up.
16 The other girl has a pant blue # the shirt blue and white.

17 She got her hair yellow.
18 The face is white.
19 There's a dog.
20 It's black and white.

While these two descriptions are of approximately equal length and degree of attention to detail, the first gives a much better gestalt of the picture, in part by making explicit the relations among the different individuals and activities depicted. Elena focuses on the actions of the children, using relative clauses or other postnominal modifiers six times (in lines 6, 9, 12, 14, 16, and 17) to clarify her references. She also expresses a complex causal relationship in lines 12 and 13, referring to a ball that would roll away if a cap were not preventing it. Carmen, in contrast, mentions only two actions ("playing baseball" in line 2 and "gonna hit the ball" in line 6) and makes no relations among the children or among the actions explicit.

Similarly, telling stories about events known to the teller but not the audience requires considerable analysis of what information must be supplied and how to organize the needed information into a form that effectively makes the teller's point. Both picture descriptions and narratives require speakers to engage in self-monitoring, to figure out on-line whether their productions are sufficiently complete and comprehensible. If speakers assess that their performances have been inadequate, they must, furthermore, invoke repair mechanisms like going back to clarify referents, repeating episodes in a simpler way, or responding to listener requests for clarification. Cazden, Michaels, and Tabors (1985) give elegant examples of first-grade children engaging in spontaneous self-repair during sharing time, which demonstrate the sophisticated monitoring skills some children have acquired by age six.

Another task that relates to literacy among school-age children is giving oral definitions for words. In administering this task, my colleagues and I have used very simple words like *donkey* and *bicycle* in order to disentangle this performance from vocabulary knowledge. Children who give formal definitions, that is, superordinate terms with appropriately restrictive relative clauses, are those who do better in reading comprehension. Again, one might well ask why this connection emerges. The explanation I favor is that the ability to provide good definitions requires analysis of one's stored knowledge; the essence of a good formal definition is that much of what one knows about the word meaning is excluded from the definition, but the crucial *defining* information is included. Consider the following definitions from a native Spanish-speaking fifth grader who reads above grade level:

Umbrella # we use # umbrella is # a thing that we use in the rainy days.
The # donkey is an animal # who carries things # on his back.

Contrast definitions of the same words from a classmate who reads below grade level:

> Umbrella is to use when it's raining.
> That's an animal. It has like # long ears.

These two sets of definitions do not differ much in terms of the information provided, though one could argue that "carrying things" is more criterial for donkeys than is "long ears." The two sets differ most strikingly, though, in the ways in which the first child organized the information into a particular, definitional form, whereas the second child sometimes omitted superordinates and juxtaposed information instead of integrating it into a single sentence. The first child typified better definers in that his definitions were relatively hesitant; dysfluencies such as he displayed are evidence that he was self-monitoring and engaging in more elaborate lexical searching and syntactic planning than characterizes his normal, fluent, conversational speech.

Putting the Model Together. The component skills most clearly and closely connected to reading—letter recognition, word recognition, and use of strategies for comprehension—are typically acquired over a relatively short period of time, and in the context of targeted instruction. One can easily see them as problem spaces for children, as evidenced by their interest in the domain as well as the occurrence of errors, frustration, and emerging reanalyses. The language skills are less constrained and well defined, thus they emerge over a much longer period; in fact, there is no clear end point even in adulthood for the acquisition of vocabulary or skills of effective communication while telling stories, giving definitions, or providing explanations. However, most adults have achieved sufficiently large vocabularies and sufficient control over the production of connected discourse that these skills can be woven into complex literacy tasks.

Children, though, are clearly making problems of the task of producing extended discourse and using sophisticated vocabulary items, as is clear from transcripts of their definitions during testing sessions, and from their attempts to tell stories or give explanations during family conversations. Consider, for example, the following definition from a fifth grader (Snow, Cancino, DeTemple, and Schley, 1991, p. 95):

> A donkey is an animal that most people use to wor // to make them work for
> them # or # to # use to ride.

One can see here from the retracings, the dysfluencies, and the self-corrections the process of trying to get this definition right. Similarly, in the following story told at the dinner table, five-year-old Jake is struggling to get his point across to his father and older brother (Blum-Kulka and Snow, 1992, pp. 200–201):

JAKE: One day we stayed that much . . . all the way from (?) it's so smelly.
FATHER: What smells?
JAKE: It's (?).
FATHER: What smells?
SAM: We don't know what you're talking about. Who what smells?
JAKE: The ice cream.
FATHER: The ice cream.
JAKE: Yeah it does.
SAM: Whose ice cream smells?
FATHER: I never smelled bad ice cream Jake.
JAKE: I smelled it.
FATHER: You did? Where?
JAKE: At school.
SAM: Oh at school.
FATHER: That's most unfortunate.
JAKE: Yeah it stinks. That's the baddest in . . .
SAM: The best or the baddest?
JAKE: The baddest.
FATHER: Not the baddest. The worst.
JAKE: The worst.

Finally, a five-year-old, who evidently thinks *chunk* is a technical term meaning something like "mouthful," must work hard to explain his meaning to his parents (Davidson, 1993, p. 86):

EVAN: Do you know what sharks' chunks weigh?
MOTHER: Sharks' what?
EVAN: When they eat it.
MOTHER: Sharks' what?
EVAN: Chunks when they eat it.
MOTHER: When they eat what?
EVAN: You know how much # when the # // their chunks weigh when the shark eats the chunk?
MOTHER: No how much does a chunk weigh?
EVAN: Fifteen pounds.
MOTHER: A chunk of . . .
FATHER: You mean that a shark can take a bite out of another fish fifteen // a fifteen-pound bite out of another fish?
MOTHER: Really?
EVAN: Uh huh.

The children's persistence and hard work to get their points across in these examples suggest that oral language skills become problem spaces in much the same way as print-related reading skills do, though perhaps at more variable ages. The examples also show how parents can help children work through their problems; Jake's father and brother hold him accountable for clarity ("What smells?" "We don't know what you're talking about, who what smells?"), truthfulness ("I never smelled bad ice cream Jake"), and conventional correctness ("Not the baddest, the worst"). Evan's mother questions him repeatedly about the way in which he is using the word *chunks,* and his father finally gives a complete, grammatical, conventional gloss for Evan's intended meaning.

The model I am proposing might be conceptualized as a weaving or braiding of various strands of fiber. The width of any strand represents the degree to which it is a problem space; once automatized, the strand becomes a smooth, even thread woven into the fabric of reading for comprehension and learning. The point of this model is as follows: In looking for the influences of family interactions on literacy development, we must consider family contributions to the full array of strands in this developmental picture.

Contribution of Interactions at Home

In discussing family contributions to a variety of the strands identified above in the model of reading presented, I draw from all three of the studies cited. Fuller descriptions of each of the studies are available in the cited sources. I focus primarily on the language strands, since others' work has paid relatively less attention to these than to the classically defined reading skills.

Vocabulary. One might expect that children in families who talk a lot have larger vocabularies. In fact, though, talking a lot might not correlate with talking in ways that introduce relatively sophisticated lexical items. Hayes and Ahrens (1988) have shown that most oral language is comprised of only about ten thousand different words; even though adults know many more than ten thousand words, they evidently tend to use certain ones over and over, reserving more sophisticated vocabulary items for writing or reading comprehension. In our work (Beals and Tabors, 1993), analyzing the speech used in the families of three- to five-year-olds, we found even fewer different words (types) in regular use: under eighty-five hundred in a corpus of over five-hundred thousand, of which just about half were neither common nor rare words, but words that were family- or child-specific. When we compared the words used in these families to lists of high-frequency words (having excluded, as well, idiosyncratic, child culture, and family-specific words such as names of relatives, acquaintances, and local places, and *Lego, Teenage Mutant Ninja Turtles,* and *Cheerios*), we found that, overall, 30 percent of the types they used are rare. Presumably, as the children in the families get older, even rarer words will be used.

The use of rare words in these families related fairly robustly to child Peabody Picture Vocabulary Test (PPVT) (receptive vocabulary) scores at age five; $r = .33$, for example, for maternal use of rare words when children were age three (Snow and Tabors, 1993). Merged family scores for use of rare words at mealtimes showed correlations of .53 when children were age three, and .43 when they were age four. It seems, then, that exposure to less common, more sophisticated vocabulary at home relates directly to children's vocabulary acquisition (see Dickinson, Cote, and Smith, this volume, for related findings from preschool exposure).

Is there something special about the families who used rarer words? One difference may be that their talk tended to be organized around topics such as explaining why people do things or how things work, rather than around food, appropriate table manners, or topics of purely personal, local interest. Dickinson and Tabors (1991) found, for example, that the percentage of explanatory talk at mealtimes correlated .61 with children's vocabularies one year later, and Snow and Kurland (in press) found that mothers' tendencies to engage in "science talk," (that is, talk about scientific processes, prediction, categorization, hypothesis formulation, and discussion of general principles like attraction and repulsion) when playing with a magnet with their five-year-olds correlated .50 to the children's PPVT scores. Certain kinds of extended discourse seem to demand the use of more complex vocabulary items.

These findings from the ongoing Home-School Study of Language and Literacy Development recall earlier findings from Snow and others (1991). In that study of second- through seventh-grade children, we tried to explain variation in four literacy outcomes (word recognition, reading comprehension, vocabulary, and writing production), using as predictors variables that all related conceptually to a notion of the family-as-educator. The family-as-educator variables that we tested included maternal education, paternal education, mother's educational expectations for the child, father's educational expectations, literacy environment of the home, parental provision of homework help, and affective pleasantness of parent-child interaction during a homeworklike task. Our expectation was that families with high values on all of these variables would have children who were doing better in school, in part because their parents were providing educational enrichment at home. When tested using regression analysis, the family-as-educator variables explained 60 percent of the variation in children's vocabulary scores. The variables maternal education, mother's educational expectations, and literacy environment of the home showed particularly high correlations with vocabulary. It is worth noting, by the way, that the same variables correlated highly with children's word recognition, which is further evidence that word recognition is to some extent dependent on vocabulary.

Telling Stories and Describing Pictures. The tasks of telling stories and describing pictures have in common the demand to produce extended text.

One might expect that children learn how to produce this kind of text by participating in opportunities at home to hear or provide extended texts, for example, opportunities at dinner to tell about their day or to listen to their parents explain something complicated. In fact, results from the home-school study confirm that this is the case; the percentage of explanatory talk at mealtimes correlated .36 to children's skill at telling a story based on pictures (DeTemple and Beals, 1991), and mothers' use of science talk in the magnet task correlated .55 (Snow and Kurland, in press). The tendency when reading a new book to supplement reading of the text and identification of the pictures with discussion of what might happen next, how the child feels about the story, and what he or she is reminded of by the story correlated .29 to children's storytelling ability. It seems, then, that opportunities to engage in extended discourse in the home build skills in producing extended discourse of precisely the type that is needed for high levels of literacy. Extended discourse emerges when talk deals with complicated events or topics; when a simple story is embellished by making connections to feelings, related events, causes, and implications; and when talk moves beyond facts to explanation, or beyond opinion to argumentation.

Definitions. As noted above, skill at manipulating the definitional genre has a strong relationship to literacy, but for reasons that are not entirely clear. Perhaps this relationship depends on the metalinguistic and analytical skills indicated by the ability to give good definitions, skills that also serve the thoughtful reader well. Whatever the reason, giving good formal definitions is a task through which social class differences emerge as early as kindergarten (Dickinson and Snow, 1987) and which is closely related to reading level for third and fifth graders (Velasco and Snow, 1993). Which activities at home help children learn this skill?

In the home-school study, we have found relationships between the percentage of mealtime talk that is explanatory and children's definitions, suggesting that cognitively challenging talk is most likely to generate skill with definitions. Watson (1989) found that parental use of superordinates during a book-reading session with two-year-olds predicted the children's formal definitions one year later—a very tidy relationship, since one feature of good formal definitions is the presence of an appropriate superordinate.

On the other hand, in the study at the United Nations International School, we found that children who spoke English at home were not better at giving formal definitions in English than those who did not, and, similarly, that native speakers of French did not give better French definitions. Variance in the quality of children's definitions was better explained by their exposure to the language of definitions in school (Snow, 1990). In other words, home factors explain definitional skill up to a certain point, but thereafter opportunities for exposure to and participation in the kinds of extended discourse about complex topics that generate definitional skill evidently are more likely to occur at school.

Conclusion

Much attention has been paid to parent-child interaction during book reading, a context in which the social interaction quite explicitly supports literacy acquisition. The approach presented here, though, clarifies the relevance to literacy development of parent-child interactions that go far beyond those centered on books and book reading. Parents and children engage in many different kinds of talk together, in the service of exchanging information, affirming mutual affection, enforcing discipline and socialization, and expressing important feelings. Within those various types of talk, there can occur opportunities for talk that require syntactic planning, careful lexical selection, making explicit cross-utterance relationships, and integration of successive utterances into a particular structure. These opportunities help children develop oral language skills that, ultimately, are extremely useful in literacy. Precisely because a large and sophisticated vocabulary, skill in producing connected discourse, and skill with specific linguistic genres are all strands that get woven into the development of literacy, family interactions that enhance those various skills directly support children as they learn to read and write.

Note

1. The following transcript codes are used in this chapter: # = pause, . . . = trailing off of speech, // = self-correction, (?) = unclear word or words.

References

Anderson, R. C., and Freebody, P. "Vocabulary Knowledge." In J. T. Guthrie (ed.), *Comprehension and Teaching: Research Reviews.* Newark, Del.: International Reading Association, 1981.

Beals, D., and Tabors, P. "Arboretum, Bureaucratic, and Carbohydrates: Preschoolers' Exposure to Rare Vocabulary at Home." Paper presented at the biennial meeting of the Society for Research in Child Development, New Orleans, Mar. 1993.

Blum-Kulka, S., and Snow, C. E. "Developing Autonomy for Tellers, Tales, and Telling in Family Narrative Events." *Journal of Narrative and Life History,* 1992, 2 (3), 187–217.

Cazden, C., Michaels, S., and Tabors, P. "Spontaneous Repairs in Sharing Time Narratives." In S. Freedman (ed.), *The Acquisition of Written Language: Revision and Response.* Norwood, N.J.: Ablex, 1985.

Davidson, R. "Oral Preparation for Literacy: Mothers' and Fathers' Conversations with Early Readers." Unpublished doctoral dissertation, Graduate School of Education, Harvard University, 1993.

DeTemple, J., and Beals, D. "Family Talk: Sources of Support for the Development of Decontextualized Language Skills." *Journal of Research in Childhood Education,* 1991, 6, 11–19.

Dickinson, D. K., and Snow, C. E. "Interrelationships Among Prereading and Oral Language Skills in Kindergartners from Two Social Classes." *Early Childhood Research Quarterly,* 1987, 2, 1–25.

Dickinson, D. K., and Tabors, P. "Early Literacy: Linkages Between Home, School, and Literacy Achievement at Age Five." *Early Childhood Research Quarterly,* 1991, 6, 30–46.

Hayes, D., and Ahrens, M. "Vocabulary Simplification for Children: A Special Case of 'Motherese'?" *Journal of Child Language,* 1988, *15,* 395–410.

Hoban, R. *Riddley Walker.* London: Picador (Pan Books), 1982.

Juel, C. "Learning to Read and Write: A Longitudinal Study of Fifty-Four Children from First Through Fourth Grades." *Journal of Educational Psychology,* 1988, *80,* 437–447.

Snow, C. E. "The Development of Definitional Skill." *Journal of Child Language,* 1990, *17,* 697–710.

Snow, C. E. "Language Proficiency: Towards a Definition." In H. Dechert and G. Appel (eds.), *A Case for Psycholinguistic Cases.* Amsterdam, The Netherlands: John Benjamins, 1991a.

Snow, C. E. "The Theoretical Basis for Relationships Between Language and Literacy in Development." *Journal of Research in Childhood Education,* 1991b, *6,* 5–10.

Snow, C. E. "What Is So Hard About Learning to Read? A Pragmatic Analysis." In J. Duchan, R. Sonnenmeier, and G. Hewitt (eds.), *Pragmatics: From Theory to Practice.* Englewood Cliffs, N.J.: Prentice Hall, in press.

Snow, C. E., Cancino, H., DeTemple, J., and Schley, S. "Giving Formal Definitions: A Linguistic or Metalinguistic Skill?" In E. Bialystok (ed.), *Language Processing and Language Awareness by Bilingual Children.* New York: Cambridge University Press, 1991.

Snow, C. E., and Dickinson, D. K. "Some Skills That Aren't Basic in a New Conception of Literacy." In A. Purves and T. Jennings (eds.), *Literate Systems and Individual Lives: Perspectives on Literacy and Schooling.* Albany: State University of New York Press, 1991.

Snow, C. E., and Kurland, B. "Sticking to the Point: Talk About Magnets as a Preparation for Literacy." In D. Hicks (ed.), *Child Discourse and Social Learning: An Interdisciplinary Perspective.* New York: Cambridge University Press, in press.

Snow, C. E., and Tabors, P. "Home Influences on the Development of Literacy-Related Language Skills." Paper presented at the biennial meeting of the Society for Research in Child Development, New Orleans, Mar. 1993.

Snow, C. E., and others. *Unfulfilled Expectations: Home and School Influences on Literacy.* Cambridge, Mass.: Harvard University Press, 1991.

Stanovitch, K. "Matthew Effects in Reading: Some Consequences of Individual Differences in the Acquisition of Literacy." *Reading Research Quarterly,* 1986, *21,* 360–406.

Velasco, P., and Snow, C. E. "Cross-Language Relationships in Oral Language Skills of Bilingual Children." Unpublished manuscript, Graduate School of Education, Harvard University, 1993.

Watson, R. "Literate Discourse and Cognitive Organization: Some Relations Between Parents' Talk and Three-Year-Olds' Thought." *Applied Psycholinguistics,* 1989, *10,* 221–236.

CATHERINE E. SNOW is Henry Lee Shattuck Professor of Education at the Graduate School of Education, Harvard University.

This chapter examines literacy development from within children's social worlds and illustrates the sociocultural dynamics through which children may negotiate a functional role for writing within their symbolic repertoires.

A Sociocultural Perspective on Symbolic Development in Primary Grade Classrooms

Anne Haas Dyson

> It has been remarked that the very essence of civilization consists of purposely building monuments so as not to forget.
> —Vygotsky (1978, p. 51)

What is distinctive about human behavior, explained Vygotsky, is our use of symbols, our tendency to construct huge concrete objects—or small marks on paper—that mediate our relationship to the world without and, at the same time, to the world within: It is symbols that link the individual mind and the collective consciousness of culture. In this chapter, the central concerns are the link between the individual child and the child collective or social world and the potential influence of that link in the development of literacy.

From the semiotic and sociocultural perspective adopted here, literacy is a cultural tool for taking action in the world; its power comes from its semiotic function: Members of a culture share common ways of infusing various forms (such as sounds, actions, marks on paper, and monuments in the park) with meaning. These symbols—these connections between forms and meanings—connect us to others and, at the same time, organize our own feelings, experiences, and thoughts.

To take a simple example, a list of items to buy at the grocery store is a tool for accomplishing social action and, at the same time, for controlling one's own memory. Or take kindergartner Anthony's monument to Martin Luther King, Jr. (MLK) (see Figure 2.1). He produced this piece during a

NEW DIRECTIONS FOR CHILD DEVELOPMENT, no. 61, Fall 1993 © Jossey-Bass Publishers study unit on the civil rights movement, including the life of MLK. Amidst talk with his friends, Anthony drew and wrote a multimedia text. His picture shows MLK giving a speech—and himself, the smaller figure in the corner, talking too. He imagined himself saying, "I am Anthony," and MLK saying, "I am Martin Luther King" and "I have a dream." Anthony wrote *I M* (am) and his own name in the conversational bubble by his drawn self, and he wrote *R* in King's, *R* being the only letter he was sure was in King's name.

Anthony's construction allowed him to participate in classroom activities and, in particular, in the social talk of his seatmates and friends. At the same time, however, it also allowed him to use cultural tools to organize his own inner response to the lesson. Anthony crossed barriers of time and space and, indeed, of life and death and located himself and MLK in the same moment, which was *his* dream, that MLK "was still alive."

The study of the development of literacy as a cultural and semiotic tool differs, in fundamental ways, from earlier approaches to child literacy. At the same time, it is consistent with recent trends in child language development. These trends entail a reconception of the child as a social being, and of the developmental process as a matter involving social negotiation (Bruner and Haste, 1987). To bring these abstract ideas into the realm of primary school children, in the following section I use Anthony's MLK piece as an object lesson, a focal point for clarifying this approach to literacy development. Then I summarize two recent qualitative studies of literacy development in classroom settings, illustrating (1) the developmental dialectic between children's use of symbolic forms—their ways of examining and shaping written forms and of integrating those forms with other media—and the functions those symbols serve in the child's social world and (2) the situated nature of that development, that is, how the interaction between the child, the symbolic media, and the social world is defined by specific cultural practices for making sense.

Studying the Development of Mediated Action in Children's Worlds

To gain insight into child writing as mediated action, researchers must situate their observations of children's writing within children's social worlds. Moreover, they must attend as well to children's entire symbolic repertoires, for children's use of writing is linked to their developmental history as symbolizers—as talkers, drawers, and players.

Focus of Developmental Analysis. Early studies of the developmental beginnings of child writing focused on the product. Influenced by the prevailing psycholinguistic views of the child as a language acquirer, and consistent with dominant developmental views of the child as a Piagetian "scientist," researchers studied early mock writing (Clay, 1975) and invented spelling (Read, 1975). They portrayed the child in a "literate" environment,

Figure 2.1. Drawing by a Kindergartner, Anthony,
of Himself and Martin Luther King, Jr.

intent on figuring out how the written system works. Such an approach directs us to pay attention to Anthony's written marks but provides limited conceptual tools for making sense of Anthony's multimedia piece as a whole, or of the ongoing social world that shaped, and was shaped by, Anthony's efforts.

From the perspective adopted here, influenced by Vygotskian perspectives, the process of becoming literate involves learning to manipulate the elements of the written system (for example, letters and words) in order to manipulate the social world in some way, to take action. The basic unit of analysis is neither word nor text but mediated action—the individual engaged in the use of the mediational system in a particular situation (for a related theoretical discussion, see Wertsch, 1991). The basic developmental question is not, What changes occur over time in children's written spellings and texts? but rather, What changes occur over time in how children use the written system to participate in culturally valued literacy activities?

Role of Diverse Media. In our society, children may initially show their understanding of the sense of a literacy activity primarily through their words and actions (for example, proudly giving a relative a picture with accompanying mock writing, while saying, "I wrote you a letter"), rather than by their manipulations of the symbolic units of written language. Indeed, young children may make minimal use of print per se in "literacy" activities, depending instead on other symbolic media such as drawing and speech. As Vygotsky (1978) argued, the development of written language does not proceed in a linear way, that is, there is not a clear continuity of forms.

Anthony, for instance, similar to other young children in our society, was interested in exploring print and in using writing in nonsymbolic ways. He enjoyed making line after line of letters, doing "homework" like the big kids. Anthony primarily used drawings and speech during "writing workshop" in his K–1 classroom; he used print at times to symbolize—to represent meaning, labeling drawn things or writing their "talk" (for example, writing "Hi" next to a drawn person). In the MLK event, Anthony's use of pictures and writing exemplifies these kinds of activities (see Figure 2.1).

The study of children over time in varied literacy activities (for example, letter writing and story composing) reveals functional shifts, as literacy begins to mediate more of the social and intellectual work earlier carried by other media. A major developmental change may be from young children's use of writing as a kind of prop, an interesting object to be used in various kinds of social and often playful activities, to the deliberate manipulation of written language as a mediator through which social activity occurs (for a review of related research, see Dyson, 1991, in press).

Role of the Peer Social World. It is through dialogue with others that children come to realize the unique functional potential of the various symbol systems in their society (Vygotsky, 1978). Interaction reveals the social desires, expectations, and even resources of symbol users. Anthony's talk with his peers during the MLK event illustrates the value of dialogue. Anthony is sitting with his kindergarten friends and classmates Lamar, Clay, and Tyler. The children, all African American, attend a racially integrated school in the center of a West Coast city. As they work, the boys talk about peace marches and the tension between white people watching a march and the marchers themselves (who, they knew, may have included white people too). The race-related topic seems to have led most of the boys to use color representationally in drawing people, although on previous occasions they, like many young children, have used color in nonsymbolic ways (Golomb, 1992). Anthony, however, is coloring MLK blue.

CLAY: [Looks at Anthony's paper and says with indignation] I'm not blue! [That is, "MLK was the same color as me, and I'm not blue!"]
ANTHONY: Huh? I just did it blue!
CLAY: They don't, they don't—
LAMAR: [In a quiet but urgent voice] Anthony, Anthony. Can't you see? Got no black!
ANTHONY: Martin Luther King—
LAMAR: Martin Luther King is not blue [stated firmly].
ANTHONY: [Picks up an orange color to fill in MLK's face] You guys are not nice. Anybody can color it anything they wanta color it.

.

.

.

ANTHONY: Martin Luther King has an R in it. How do you spell Martin Luther King? [No child at the table is sure.]

Anthony did not manipulate color in a representationally significant way, and this disrupted the sense of social solidarity that had been evident in the children's talk. Anthony could use the available symbolic media to express himself as an individual, but to be realized, that expression had to be acknowledged by others. In this case, that realization was made problematic because of the symbolic potential and cultural meanings of color.

In a similar way, Anthony's capacity as an individual to gain control over the written system in particular activities is inextricably linked to his participation in a social world in which such activity is important. To learn a mediational tool, including talk or writing, children need other people who not only model and guide the appropriate processes but also respond to their efforts (their spoken words, written texts, drawings and paintings) in situationally and culturally appropriate ways. It is those responses that imbue the child's symbolic acts with social meaning, and it is, in turn, the sense of a functional goal that organizes and drives the symbolic process.

In securing such responses, peers may be particularly valuable. Many children's symbolic and, more generally, communicative skills develop through peer interaction (Ervin-Tripp, 1991; Hartup, 1983), perhaps because children more easily negotiate with peers than with their teachers. Although adults serve many critically important roles in children's written language learning, from modeling to direct assistance, it may be relatively easier for children to function as true addresses for each other's writing.

Teachers must focus on their instructional goals, and their efforts to teach may limit the kinds of responses they offer children (see Daiute, Campbell, Griffin, Reddy, and Tivnan, this volume; Tizard and Hughes, 1984). Through informal interaction among peers, children may learn not only how to elicit others' attention and approval through their texts but also how to manipulate others' responses for different ends, that is, how to negotiate relationships with others through the mediational tool of writing. The ways in which young children learn to interact socially through written texts was a focus of the research project summarized in the following section.

Dialectic Between Symbolic Form and Function in the Children's Worlds

In a longitudinal study conducted at an urban magnet school of eighty students, I observed the changing role of writing in four- to eight-year-old children's story composing and social interaction during a daily composing period (Dyson, 1989). The children in this small primary school had the same three teachers, including the same language arts teacher, from kindergarten through third grade. As part of their language arts period, all children had a daily journal time, in which they often composed imaginative stories; the kindergarten children dictated, but, by first grade, all children wrote (as well as drew and talked). The journals were central objects in the culture of the school; all completed journals were displayed in the school library before they were taken home to be shared with parents.

The journal writing of eight key children was the focus of my research. The children were, in almost all cases, from working-class homes and were selected in part because they seemed relatively dependent on the school for literacy learning (for an illustration of the pedagogical link between early literacy experiences in and out of school, see Dyson, 1990). Like most of their classmates, the children initially "wrote" primarily by drawing and talking. With those tools, they not only represented their ideas and expressed their feelings but also connected with their friends; children talked about and at times playfully dramatized one another's drawn and told stories. As in Anthony's MLK piece, their actual writing was only a small part of their multimedia productions.

The study identified the challenges that the children faced in accomplishing through story writing what they had earlier done through drawing and talking. There were artistic tensions between drawing, talking, and writing, tensions created by differences in the space and time conventions of these diverse media and also by the unidimensional nature of written language, which demands words for dramatized gestures and qualities of voice. These tensions were evident in the children's talk during composing and also in their texts (for example, in shifts of tense and of person).

The precise nature of the challenges that individual children faced in learning to write depended in part on their particular artistic styles. For instance, some children enacted dramatic adventures as they drew, capturing fast motorcycles and life-threatening gun battles in swirls and jagged lines. To illustrate, kindergartner Jesse drew a "motorcycle guy" swirling around a race track, crashing and then swirling again. As he drew, he dramatized and narrated the present-tense actions of the guy, intermittently making the sound of a gunned motor. He then dictated, "This is the motorcycle guy [a description of his picture, which indeed exists in the present tense]. And then the motorcycle guy won [a record of past told and dramatized action]." Jesse's dramatic actions and voice did not appear in his written text, and the accumulated actions piled on his drawing did not easily spread out in written words.

Kindergartner Regina, on the other hand, drew not dramatic actions but scenes of little girls, suns, flowers, and small animals. She talked elaborately about each figure she drew, and so numerous potential narratives evolved as she filled her page. For example, "And now I'm gonna make a Cabbage Patch Kid [a kind of doll]. And this is the bird that's flying him to the hospital. . . . And this little girl she's gonna jump out of the balloon and try to land on the red heart. And if she gets on it, she wins a surprise." When Regina was done, she had "much much much" going on in her pictures and therefore many stories to "write"; her initial strategy was simply to describe the dominant characters in her picture, its static frame freezing in time and space figures caught in many separate plots. For example, for her picture of girls, a Cabbage Patch Kid, and birds, she described only the girls: "These little girls are standing."

As children began to attend to each other's writing, their playful and critical talk engulfed their texts, just as it did their drawing, making the texts legitimate objects of reflection, separate from their pictures. The children began to consider critically the relationships between their pictures and their texts. Gradually, the children began to assume greater control of the kind of information they would include in each medium. Their written stories contained more narrative action, their pictures more illustrations of key ideas.

Moreover, they began to use writing to accomplish social work, that is, to maintain and manipulate their relationships with peers. Their friends became characters in their written stories, and they also began to plan to include certain words or actions to amuse or tease them. Thus, their words became mediational tools, in part, at least, because the words began to serve multiple functions within their social lives. That is, over time, writing allowed the children to make connections with, and writing became more embedded in, their social lives.

For example, as first-grader Mitzi sat and talked with her friends, she drew and then wrote quick formulaic texts. Although, unlike Regina, she did not talk about her drawings, she too drew scenes of little girls, rainbows, clouds, and hearts. After she drew a picture, Mitzi wrote a variant of "Once upon a time there was a . . . ," followed by a label for the drawn figure and then a proclamation of affection, or lack thereof ("I love this [drawn figure]"). The form of Mitzi's written stories, however, like the story forms of all of the children observed, was directly influenced by—and in turn influenced—her ongoing social life. In Vygotskian terms, her written text was infused with social meaning in the external peer social world, and this, in turn, guided her internal considerations.

To illustrate, I compare two "witch stories," one from the first grade, one from the second grade. In the first grade, Mitzi drew a "mean-looking witch," with which she was very pleased. The witch was, she said, her all-time "favorite story." After drawing, she wrote, "Once there was a witch. She is my mom. I love my mom." Mitzi's friends, Jenni and Bessi, were sitting nearby and overheard their friend as she mouthed and reread the words she was spelling.

BESSI: You shouldn't share it [with the class].
MITZI: She's a bad witch [pointing to her picture].
JENNI: Then you're a bad girl.

Perhaps a little girl who writes that her own mother is a witch is a bad child indeed, from Jenni's point of view. Mitzi seemed to interpret Jenni's statement similarly: "No, I'm not. I might not even like my mom, or I love my mom." At this point, Mitzi drew a conversation bubble next to her drawn witch and wrote: "I am bad."

In this event, Mitzi's labeling of her mother as a witch conflicted with loving her mother, which made Mitzi's readers (her friends) uncomfortable. Like Anthony's blue MLK, Mitzi's mother witch entered into a dialectic with the social life around it, a dialectic that highlighted the symbolic potential and social consequences of composing acts.

A year later, Mitzi composed another witch story while sitting by her friend Jenni. Reflecting general changes in the dynamics of all of the observed children's writing, Mitzi now used her writing more deliberately as a social tool. While her drawing, which now followed rather than preceded writing, still contained more details of character and mood, it was writing that advanced Mitzi's plot. She put both herself and her friend Jenni in the story. In fact, Jenni was the witch. Moreover, she used her text to engage with—to manipulate—her friend.

MITZI: [To Jenni] Now this is going to be true dream.

MITZI: This is a nightmare I once had and the girl was you.
JENNI: Yeah?
MITZI: And you really hated me.
JENNI: No wonder it's a nightmare.

Mitzi's completed text vacillates between past and present, reflecting her own movement between imagined past and present social world:

> I had a dream and My dream was a BiG NiGhtMare. and This is My Nightmare. Once there was a Girl and her name was Jenni and she hated Me. But I do not know why. and she has a magic bulb. her bulb was a very powerful bulb. It was so powerful it turned Me into a Powerful bulb and now she has Two Powerfull Bulbs. The one that is Me is even Powerfuller than the other one. The End.

As soon as she finished, Mitzi turned to Jenni and said, "Okay, want me to read this to you? It's very funny." Mitzi then drew an accompanying picture, in which Jenni has a witchlike nose and hands and is saying, "He, he." Jenni, while examining Mitzi's picture, said, "That's not very nice." But Mitzi was prepared to defend herself and her story by referring to its genre: "But this is my nightmare!"

To summarize the nature of the developmental changes illustrated, first-grader Mitzi orchestrated—drew on her knowledge of written language—to participate in the daily journal time. But that orchestration was negotiated through the use of alternative kinds of symbols and with the support of other people. Indeed, writing was more prop than mediator. However, those very resources posed developmental challenges. In her classroom social life, Mitzi's text became a point of attention (and contention), and that attention supported her own critical reflection on meanings drawn, written, and spoken and on the relationship between her own actions and the responses of others.

As she gained experience with written language, Mitzi responded to these productive tensions between media and between people by using her symbolic and social resources in new, more text-dependent ways. For example, she transformed talkative friends into story characters and used drawings to illustrate key written ideas. Her ways of examining and shaping symbolic forms were influenced by—and influenced—the nature of the evolving social and symbolic life of the wider community of children. That is, for all of the children, not just for Mitzi, writing was becoming a valued medium, and this value was reinforced by the larger culture of the school. As Mitzi's witch stories illustrated, loving and hating now could occur both on and off the page, and the artistic world, ongoing social world, and wider, experienced world were linked in a dynamic dialectic.

Mitzi's last anecdote contained a reference to a genre (the nightmare), and that reference suggests a specificity to the developmental study of mediated action in the children's world, a specificity I have recently begun to address. That is, children are not simply learning to interact in a generic way through written language; rather, they are learning to engage in particular kinds of social relationships through the written medium, as illustrated in the study discussed below.

Situated Nature of Symbolic Development

From the theoretical perspective adopted here, there is no culturally neutral developmental process through which children acquire written language. As Ferdman (1990) discussed, since literacy involves the manipulation of symbols that represent cultural meanings (for example, the word *witch*), and since the manipulation must happen in culturally appropriate ways, the process of becoming literate is also a process of becoming a cultural member (see also Heath, 1983; Ochs, 1988).

Children's use of the mediational tools of language is shaped by their participation in speech and literacy events in their homes and communities. Thus, they bring to school a repertoire of genres or familiar ways of using language. As Morson (1986, p. 89) explained in discussing Bakhtin, each genre "temporarily crystallize[s] a network of relations" between the speakers and other people. For example, children come to understand how people tell jokes, to whom, and about what. They may learn, for instance, that teasing one's sister by casting her as a character in a scatological joke is more fun than teasing one's mother in a similar way (Dunn, 1988). A child's use of any genre, then, involves more than simply producing a kind of discourse. It involves assuming a certain stance toward other people and toward the world.

Children's repertoires of genres become the resources on which they draw in school literacy tasks. Children orchestrate their symbolic resources—and, if allowed, produce their multimedia texts—in order to achieve particular social goals. Therefore, learning to write in school involves figuring out, and gaining entry into, the range of social dialogues enacted through literacy, including the assumed relationships between writers and their audiences.

This is a complex process, since schools are not homogeneous cultural worlds. Although the teacher governs the official school world, in which children must be students, the children are also members of an unofficial peer world, formed in response to the constraints and regulations of the official world, and they are members as well of their sociocultural communities, which may re-form in the classroom amidst networks of peers (D'Amato, 1987).

Within each world, children have different kinds of relationships to one another and to their teacher; moreover, they enact those relationships through intersecting but nonetheless distinctive ways of using language. To elaborate, any one language is composed of "a multitude of concrete worlds" (Bakhtin, 1981, p. 288), each world with its own social beliefs and language values. These social spheres exist because of varied kinds of stratification, including those for particular age groups, ethnic groups, and disciplines. All of these groups have their own ways of using language. Interwoven with such social stratification is generic stratification, a repertoire of ways of speaking and writing in particular situations.

The social spheres of interest here—the official school world, the unofficial peer world, and the sociocultural community as realized in the classroom—do not always agree on appropriate genre themes, structures, and styles (see, for example, Cazden, 1988; Heath, 1983). To achieve their social ends, children may draw on ethnic or folk genres that they share with certain class members, popular genres shared widely in the peer world, or written literary genres shared in the official school world.

In a recent study (Dyson, in press), I examined the range of social goals that energized young children's composing, the kinds of discourse traditions on which they drew to achieve those ends, and the ways in which they differentiated and negotiated among the complex social worlds of their classroom. The site of the study was an urban K–3 school in the east San Francisco Bay Area. Demographically, the school served mainly two neighborhoods: 52 percent of the children came from an African American neighborhood and the others from an integrated but primarily European American neighborhood; about 27 percent of the children were Anglo, and there were small percentages of children from many different heritages.

Focusing on six key children, kindergartners through third graders, all African American, I constructed discourse maps of each child's school life, paying attention to how children used various kinds of texts to enact and negotiate diverse social relationships with others. For example, a dominant social goal in children's as well as adults' worlds is to establish social cohesion. To achieve this goal with their peers, the children often drew on material from popular culture: stories about superheroes, verses by rap stars, or scenes from horror movies. Such material was apt to elicit an "Oh yeah, I saw that too" from a child addressee, or a "Me too, I like that too." Third-grader Ayesha, for instance, wrote a list of rap stars seen on the Grammy Awards show. During rug time sharing, her piece was enthusiastically received: "M. C. Hammer, yes! Bobby Brown, yes!"

All of the observed children also composed to engage in artful performances, through which they hoped to gain others' attention and respect. They often drew on their oral folk resources (that is, features of verbal art, which highlight the musical and image-creating properties of language; see Smitherman, 1986; Tannen, 1989), and they also tended to explicitly manipulate their texts; for example, they tried to make words rhyme, phrases rhythmic, dialogue fast-paced, and images funny. The aim was not a confirming "me too" but a pleased and, maybe, surprised "Oh!" or even laughter.

First-grader Jameel was an especially dramatic performer. To accompany drawn and dramatized adventures, he wrote dialogue and rhythmic chants, just as did some of his favorite children's authors (like Dr. Seuss). For example, one text was about two friends, Cat and Hat, who alternately sat on each other—until Cat was run over by a car and Hat called 911:

> Sat on Cat. Sat on Hat.
> Hat Sat on CAT.
> CAT GoN. 911 for CAt

Jameel looked forward to performing his stories and showing his pictures to an appreciative audience during sharing time. During the year, he wrote pop songs and jokes, as well as more proselike stories. Like all of the observed children, when performing Jameel did not appreciate help from audience members.

Jameel seldom wrote simply to present others with necessary information; but like the other observed children, when given opportunities *to teach or explain information,* he did so orally. Jameel was careful and relatively explicit in his speech, although he often used humor and metaphorical language as explanatory tools. In the following excerpt, he taught me about birds (transcription code # = pause):

> We got lots of bird books. Would you like to read one of 'em? [Jameel gets a bird alphabet book; he skips the pages that his teacher read that morning because] these are the things you already know about because you was here. # This bird is very interesting. It eats little kinds of beans. # Let's see. This one is a dentist. [The dentist metaphor is Jameel's, not his teacher's.] This is a crocodile bird that cleans out the little stuff stuck up in his teeth. [This assertion is accurate.] The crocodiles will never eat him. They will never eat their dentist. # Now this, is a duck. # It's a member of the duck family.

The situated nature of young children's writing, that is, the enactment in particular settings informed by specific social goals, makes problematic certain pedagogical assumptions about child writing. First, the instructional literature often assumes that the developmental goal is "decontextualized" written language (for example, Olson, 1984), that is, language in which ideas are made explicit in tightly constructed prose, rather than implicitly understood by familiar interlocutors. But given that written language always exists within a kind of social relationship, so-called decontextualized language also exists only in certain situational and textual contexts, that is, in certain genres. For example, most of the observed children produced such language when they were teaching a needy other. Moreover, children can begin writing by producing a diversity of genres, and any one child may control diverse sorts of texts. In complex societies such as ours, the most valuable developmental and instructional outcome is not children's control of any one kind of genre or style but their ability to be flexible in discourse use, to understand the social and political or power implications of the various uses of language.

Second, the pedagogical literature was tended to assume that certain kinds of "writing workshop" social arrangements (for instance, teacher and peer conferences; see Graves, 1983) are interpreted in the same way by all children. For example, teachers are encouraged to arrange social situations in which child composers receive helpful "responses" from "authentic" peer audiences. But a teacher's "whole group writing conference" might be a peer occasion for social cohesion or a child's show-time stage, in both of which an explicitly helpful audience would be inappropriate (just as it is in our common culture).

To consider children as social actors is thus to suggest that *audience, editor,* and *response* are situated, not generic, terms that can be explicitly discussed and planned for with children. This perspective suggests as well the importance of diverse situations for composing. To produce certain kinds of texts, children must understand the social work that text is intended to accomplish. Thus, educators may need to create occasions for guided writing beyond open-ended composing periods, when diverse purposes and audiences can be socially negotiated and made socially sensible for and with children (see Gray, 1987).

Summary: Children's Textual Monuments

Like kindergartner Anthony, third-grader Ayesha was inspired by the study of the civil rights movement and MLK. She wrote a piece to perform for her peers; through his monument, she organized her inspiration into words and also proclaimed it for her peers:

> Martin Luther King was a preacher.
> He really knew how to talk.
> In August he led a peace march.
> He walked and walked and walked.
> One day they threw a bomb at his house. It was bigger than a mouse.
> The KKK was very bad.
> . They made the people very mad, and also made them sad.
> He was a serious man
> and taught peace on the land.

What are the developmental roots of such textual monuments? They are not to be found simply in early scribbles. Rather, they are found in children's efforts to orchestrate all of their symbolic resources—including pictures, spoken words, and dramatic movement—for the artful declaration of self, for the presentation of images, sounds, and actions. The mechanisms accounting for change involve not only the internal drive to more effectively express intentions but also the external cultural world, which provides models, guidance, and an engaging social life in which the children, and their monuments, figure.

In sum, children do not invent written language; they negotiate its use in particular circumstances with particular others, supported by other media and, often, by other children. To understand and better support child learners, we need to attend, then, not simply to written marks on a page but also to mediated acts in the world.

References

Bakhtin, M. M. "Discourse in the Novel." In *The Dialogic Imagination: Four Essays by M. Bakhtin.* (C. Emerson and M. Holquist, trans.) Austin: University of Texas Press, 1981.

Bruner, J., and Haste, H. (eds.). *Making Sense: The Child's Construction of the World.* New York: Methuen, 1987.

Cazden, C. *Classroom Discourse: The Language of Teaching and Learning.* Portsmouth, N.H.: Heinemann Educational Books, 1988.

Clay, M. *What Did I Write?* Portsmouth, N.H.: Heinemann Educational Books, 1975.

D'Amato, J. D. "The Belly of the Beast: On Cultural Difference, Castelike Status, and the Politics of School." *Anthropology and Education Quarterly,* 1987, *18,* 357–360.

Dunn, J. *The Beginnings of Social Understandings.* Cambridge, Mass.: Harvard University Press, 1988.

Dyson, A. H. *Multiple Worlds of Child Writers: Friends Learning to Write.* New York: Teachers College Press, 1989.

Dyson, A. H. "Weaving Possibilities: Rethinking Metaphors for Early Literacy Development." *The Reading Teacher,* 1990, *44,* 202–213.

Dyson, A. H. "The Word and the World: Reconceptualizing Written Language Development." *Research in the Teaching of English,* 1991, *25,* 97–123.

Dyson, A. H. *Social Worlds of Children Learning to Write in an Urban Primary School.* New York: Teachers College Press, in press.

Ervin-Tripp, S. "Play in Language Development." In B. Scales, M. Almy, A. Nicolopoulou, and S. Ervin-Tripp (eds.), *Play and the Social Context of Development in Early Care and Education.* New York: Teachers College Press, 1991.

Ferdman, B. "Literacy and Cultural Identity." *Harvard Educational Review,* 1990, *60,* 181–204.

Golomb, C. *The Child's Creation of a Pictorial World.* Berkeley: University of California Press, 1992.

Graves, D. H. *Writing: Teachers and Children at Work.* Portsmouth, N.H.: Heinemann Educational Books, 1983.

Gray, B. "How Natural Is 'Natural' Language Teaching: Employing Wholistic Methodology in the Classroom." *Australian Journal of Early Childhood,* 1987, *12,* 3–19.

Hartup, W. W. "Peer Relations." In P. H. Mussen (ed.), *Handbook of Child Psychology.* Vol. 4: *Socialization, Personality, and Social Development.* (4th ed.) New York: Wiley, 1983.

Heath, S. B. *Ways with Words: Language, Life, and Work in Communities and Classrooms.* New York: Cambridge University Press, 1983.

Morson, G. S. "Introduction to Extracts from 'The Problem of Speech Genres.' " In G. S. Morson (ed.), *Bakhtin: Essays and Dialogues on His Work.* Chicago: University of Chicago Press, 1986.

Ochs, E. *Culture and Language Development: Language Acquisition and Language Socialization in a Samoan Village.* New York: Cambridge University Press, 1988.

Olson, D. " 'See! Jumping!' Some Oral Language Antecedents of Literacy." In H. Goelman, A. Oberg, and F. Smith (eds.), *Awakening to Literacy*. Portsmouth, N.H.: Heinemann Educational Books, 1984.

Read, C. *Children's Categorizations of Speech Sounds in English*. Urbana, Ill.: National Council of Teachers of English, 1975.

Smitherman, G. *Talkin' and Testifyin': The Language of Black America*. Detroit: Wayne State University Press, 1986.

Tannen, D. *Talking Voices: Repetition, Dialogue, and Imagery in Conversational Discourse*. New York: Cambridge University, 1989.

Tizard, B., and Hughes, M. *Young Children Learning*. Cambridge, Mass.: Harvard University Press, 1984.

Vygotsky, L. S. *Mind in Society: The Development of Higher Psychological Processes*. (M. Cole, V. John-Steiner, S. Scribner, and E. Souberman, eds.) Cambridge, Mass.: Harvard University Press, 1978.

Wertsch, J. V. *Voices of the Mind: A Sociocultural Approach to Mediated Action*. Cambridge, Mass.: Harvard University Press, 1991.

ANNE HAAS DYSON is professor of education in language and literacy at the University of California, Berkeley.

A contrastive analysis of teacher-student and peer collaborations reveals diverse approaches to writing. Results of this study suggest that children draw on social and affective resources to support cognitive and linguistic aspects of written language development.

Young Authors' Interactions with Peers and a Teacher: Toward a Developmentally Sensitive Sociocultural Literacy Theory

Colette Daiute, Carolyn H. Campbell, Terri M. Griffin, Maureen Reddy, Terrence Tivnan

This chapter outlines theoretical issues in the social construction of literacy, focusing on the role of expertise, talk, and activity. We contrast children's interactions with a teacher, who models expert literacy strategies, and interactions among young peers, whose spontaneous strategies differ from those of the teacher but are nonetheless effective as instructional supports, especially for some children. Our study illustrates how children's active engagement with peers around written texts can be more important for certain aspects of literacy development than access to an expert. These results suggest that literacy development is a complex process, involving social and affective factors as well as cognitive factors like expert planning strategies and knowledge. Teachers and other experts can instruct children on culturally privileged features of literacy, but children must have opportunities to integrate these features into their own diverse, spontaneous oral and written genres. Children's effective manipulation of text forms appears to be centered on meaning making, personal connections, and social contexts, as well as on the cognitive and linguistic processes that have dominated research and practice.

The research reported in this chapter was supported by the National Council of Teachers of English Research Foundation and Harvard University Graduate School of Education.

Role of Social Interaction in Literacy Development

In recent years, there has been emphasis on understanding the role of social interaction in the development of literacy and other problem-solving domains, but individual researchers have construed social interaction in diverse ways, as evidenced in the chapters in this book. Some theorists and educators emphasize the value of expert collaborators guiding children to do more complex problem solving than they would engage in on their own (Collins, Brown, and Newman, 1989). Other researchers emphasize the dialogic nature of thought in the context of social interaction and children's active engagement when working with peers (Daiute and Dalton, 1993; Dyson, 1989; Nystrand and Gamoran, 1991; Nystrand, Greene, and Wiemelt, in press). In this chapter, we focus on the contrast between social reproduction as characterized in a teacher's modeling of expert composing strategies and social construction as characterized by collaboration among young novice writers in an urban setting. Such a contrast offers insights about relationships between social formations of mind and other factors within individuals, like developmental and affective factors, which typically have not been integrated into cognitive developmental or social interactionist theories.

Expertise. One of Vygotsky's major contributions to educational research has been the concept of "zone of proximal development," which is the distance between a child's actual level of development as assessed when working individually on a task and the child's potential level of development as assessed when working "under adult guidance or in collaboration with more capable peers" (Vygotsky, 1978, p. 86). According to this theory, a child performs at a higher developmental level with a partner who has extensive knowledge and who can model the culturally accepted way of doing a task. Drawing on their knowledge and skill, experts can engage children in performing at higher levels of abstraction and performance than they would achieve individually. Experts reveal knowledge and skills, assess and guide the novice's participation, and gradually transfer control of the activity to the novice in response to the novice's increasing competence (Rogoff, 1990).

In the following excerpt, for example, a teacher is collaborating with her student to compose a story based in the social studies curriculum. This teacher is guiding eight-year-old Gary to use the composing strategy of writing an opening sentence that will engage a reader. Previous research has shown that experienced writers compose with frequent reference to such planning strategies, but children do not.[1]

TEACHER: Got it! What a good idea you have! Now we need a catcher sentence at the beginning, that's going to get everybody to want to read this story in the newspaper!

GARY: Hmm.

TEACHER: What was significant? What was the most important thing about the printing press? Why was that an important invention?

GARY: It made it easy, it made it easier to copy things, like umm you wouldn't have to write every page or something. Or if you wanted to have copies, you could just put it on the printing press, and it would go easier.

TEACHER: Right. And then people could # could, and then more ideas could spread, because people could write down their ideas and pass it along.

GARY: Mm-hmm.

Trying to move beyond mere transmittal models of education, this teacher collaborates with her student so that he can participate in her expert strategies, use language related to them, and apply strategies interactively with the teacher as a basis for using them later on his own.

Talking around a challenging task with an expert may be a catalyst to development because of the more complex nature of the expert's speech. When a child collaborates with an expert, the expert asks questions, names concepts as well as physical objects (Wood and Middleton, 1975), and engages in other verbalization that sparks the child's recognition and understanding of abstract concepts related to the activity. Such talk presumably focuses children on the salient aspects of a task, makes connections between different parts of a task, and offers appropriate labels that may serve as aids to synthesis or memory. Expert-guided talk has been described as *scaffolding* (Wood and Middleton, 1975). The scaffolding metaphor highlights an external structure, which is emphasized in much instruction, to hold in place a weaker structure that is destined to be shaped in ways prescribed by the scaffold. Scaffolding has been shown to be effective for supporting literacy development (Palincsar and Brown, 1984), but mostly for older children (Bereiter and Scardamalia, 1987). Nevertheless, sometimes scaffolds are ill-matched to the organic nature of the action and thought that children bring to instruction. Children's failure to benefit from even the best instruction may be attributable to inappropriate scaffolding, scaffolding that cannot accommodate how children make sense of phenomena, problems, and possibilities in the world around them.

Collaborative Problem Solving Through Talk and Activity by Peers. Although a teacher might offer children expert strategies, children typically have the opportunity to talk about ideas and problems more spontaneously and more critically when working with equally novice peers. In fact, the children in our study spoke more when they worked with peers on collaborative writing activities than when they worked with the teacher: 865 words on average for each child in peer collaboration compared to 571.8 words in a similar amount of time when working with the teacher. Children's increased conversation around ideas represents increased engagement with and control over ideas, since children typically need to be actively engaged, and speech is a minds-on (like hands-on) activity. According to Vygotsky (1978), speech is crucial to development because it mediates a relationship between the speaker's knowledge and the object of the collaborative action—whether it is solving a memory problem, playing a game, or writing a story. When engaged in collaborative problem solving with a peer, a child not only has the opportunity to talk but also may be freer to take intellectual risks. Compare, for example, the earlier excerpt of the conversation between Gary and his teacher to the following excerpt from eight-year-olds Andy and Russ's conversation, which reflects their mutual orientation, experimentation, and meaning making.

1 ANDY: I # Spaniard Christopher Columbus rediscovered the West Indies thinking it was Japan # But it really # oops!
2 RUSS: He met, he met new people.
3 ANDY: When it really was # oh, wait, but it really was umm # think-um, America. Is America . . .
4 RUSS: Didn't Amarigold [Amerigo Vespucci] come before Christopher Columbus, to America?
5 ANDY: No. But he rediscovered it, though.
6 RUSS: Then it can't, can't be America # then you can't, then he could // then you shouldn't write.
7 ANDY: He rediscovered it.
8 RUSS: Yeah.
9 ANDY: The Indians discovered it first.
10 RUSS: But # the West Indie, but he didn't realize that the West . . .
11 ANDY: No, but wait, wait.
12 RUSS: Yeah.
13 ANDY: But it, but it, but it really was America. See, it's North America.
14 RUSS: Well, okay. This could be, umm, from the future?! Not really like a . . .
15 ANDY: Oh, ya, we don't // oh, yeah, this is // Oh, yeah, we're # oh [raspberry] forget me.
16 RUSS: Who?
17 ANDY: Ya, we're the people with the Medicis.

In contrast to the excerpt between Gary and his teacher, this exchange between Andy and Russ is characterized by interdependence: The boys do not act on previous plans but work into an intellectual course of action that depends on their interaction. What each child says has immediate creative consequences, as they listen and adjust their thinking, as shown especially in utterances 3 through 9. This interaction is also characterized by meaning making; the boys are trying to figure out a time sequence and the related perceptions of Christopher Columbus. As they draw on their knowledge about Columbus's voyages and about places and people in the world during the Renaissance, they propose ideas about where Columbus thought he was, what he might have called the place where he landed. These children's intellectual inquiry evolves as they create a story, recognize a problem, and address this problem through social interaction. As they conjecture, debate, and follow ideas interdependently, their composing process and text take shape. Such intuitive planning contrasts markedly with expert strategies as reported in much cognitive science research (Collins, Brown, and Newman, 1989), yet interactive planning appears to be quite effective for some children (Daiute, 1989; Daiute and Dalton, 1988, 1993).

The activity of the interaction is also important, not only as a focal point but also for its role in supporting the thinking process. When Andy and Russ, for example, tried to refer to the place where Columbus and his crew landed, they needed a name for it. Having to decide on the name involved them in a discussion about historical issues like which people had been there already (utterances 4, 6, and 9). This kind of activity with text, as with objects like tools and toys, is crucial to the developmental process because children's collective labor around the object engages them in thinking about it. As they work with text, collaborators examine and analyze the characteristics and functions of the object and its relationships to other objects. The tasks of proposing concepts and phrases to a partner, discussing those text sequences, revising, and building on text fragments increase children's experience with text and their reflection on it. Experience with text and metalinguistic awareness have been reported to be key components of literacy achievement.

Although novice peers may have equally unsophisticated speech in relation to a task, their talk and activity appear to engage them in cognitions that advance their knowledge and performance (Daiute and Dalton, 1988, 1993). Since expertise, talk, and activity have not been compared in different types of collaborations, we do not know about either the different or the complementary effects of having access to an expert or having a partner with whom one can discuss intellectual material in concrete exploratory terms. Our study was designed to compare expert-novice and peer collaboration as a way of identifying factors pertinent to the development of literacy theory.

Goals and Research Questions

The goal of the study was to learn about how children approach literacy tasks in the context of social interaction with peers and with a teacher. The idea behind this study was that if literacy is a social process, then social interaction may be an optimum context in which to develop and practice literacy. Social interaction among peers, moreover, may motivate children, especially those eight years of age and older, who focus intensely on their peer group. In addition, when working with peers, children may use their spontaneous approaches to tasks, including action, thought, and language that are developmentally appropriate.

In addition to exploring literacy in the context of social interaction to gain insights about how children make sense of written language and literacy tasks, a goal of this study was to determine whether and how these diverse social interactions related to changes in children's writing over time. The following questions guided our research: What is the nature of social interaction as children engage in challenging literacy activities with a peer and with a teacher? What are the strategies that children use? What do children choose as their curriculum when they compose collaboratively with a peer? How do the spontaneous curricula and social interaction processes of children working with peers and with the teacher relate to changes in children's individual writing over time?

Research Context. The data described here are from a year-long study that took place in an open third- and fourth-grade classroom in a desegregated, urban school that is known throughout the city system for student diversity, developmental teaching, teacher involvement, innovation, and excellence. The teacher had been recommended by the city's elementary language arts coordinator as someone who structures and invites a variety of types of collaboration. We wanted to study the nature and value of socially mediated literacy development in a context where the teachers and students were familiar with collaboration so that we would not be witnessing problems or successes with collaborative work that were the result of inexperience or novelty.

The teacher's curriculum was challenging, interdisciplinary, and coherent. Reading, writing, mathematics, and science are built around a social studies curriculum designed to immerse children in the Middle Ages, the Renaissance, the Exploration, and the Mayans. In addition to reading and writing activities, children had multisensory experiences with each curriculum area, such as creating, staging, and performing a puppet show set in the Middle Ages, role-playing characters such as Renaissance guild members by preparing and selling their wares at a Renaissance fair, and participating in a simulated archeological dig to discover the Mayan civilization. Writing experiences included fairy tales, fairy tale mathematical problems, journals of a person traveling in Columbus's ship, research papers about the Mayans, and stories. Parents as well as other children and teachers participated in events to share the children's intellectual and artistic work, and the children's writing was displayed at fairs and celebrations as well as in the classroom and library. Thus, children had many opportunities to write and to share their writing in the school community. Writing instruction occurred mostly in teacher-student conferences and occasionally through group instruction on how to organize the research-writing process and how to comment on peers' writing (Graves, 1983).

Participants. The head classroom teacher, Ann, is a confident, experienced, energetic teacher who has high expectations and compassion for her students. She is a European American woman, mother of three, and has taught in the school for several years.

Ann's students represent a wide range of abilities, cultural and ethnic backgrounds (five African Americans, one Asian American, one Indian American, and nine European Americans), and economic groups (range from low to high income across groups). The sixteen children in the study scored from 2.7 to 12.0 grade equivalent on the mixed language section of the California Achievement Test in the same year of the study. Because of the intensive nature of this study in terms of the number of writing sessions by each child over time (nine), the number of forty-five minute conversations (four), texts, and interviews, we worked with only one class.

Writing Activities. Ann collaborated with our research team to create writing activities that were consistent with her curriculum and that would allow us to observe different types of collaborations in relation to children's individual writing over time. The students created a newsletter, *Time Traveler News,* in which they reported on current events in the school and historic events in the Renaissance, each of which they viewed as newsworthy. Given the curriculum and students' generally high level of interest in it, *Time Traveler News* provided a meaningful context for the children's literacy activities and a framework in which we could monitor the development of collaborative and individual writing in one genre (the news story) over time. The children were told that the newspaper would be published and distributed to them, their parents, and the other third- and fourth-grade students at the end of the project. All writing was done on the computer, so children were able to customize the final newspaper, adding to the meaningfulness of the task.

Exhibit 3.1 shows the pattern of individual and collaborative writing activities. Historical and current stories were paired in case there was a difference in children's engagement with the topics. From January into June, each student wrote with the teacher, with a peer, and individually for *Time Traveler News.*

We audiotaped and transcribed the teacher-student and peer collaboration sessions as data for our study on collaboration processes. We also collected all individual and collaborative writing samples for the newsletter.

Data Analyses. Several types of data were used for this study. For each child, there are two transcripts of teacher-student collaborative writing sessions, two transcripts of peer collaborative writing sessions, four texts from collaborative writing sessions, five texts written individually before and after each type of collaboration, and one interview. In addition, field notes about the teacher's and children's interactions in the broader classroom structure are used to provide context for the microanalyses. Two extended interviews with the teacher provide information from the teacher's point of view.

Talk Analyses. Tape recordings of conversations during collaborations were transcribed and analyzed to identify patterns of interaction and relationships between talk and text. The coding and analysis involved a corpus of forty-eight transcripts: thirty-two transcripts of teacher-student collaborative composing sessions and sixteen transcripts of collaborative composing sessions by children working in pairs. The children's transcripts range in speaking turns from 149 to 325, in utterances (identified as independent clauses, with dependent clauses and related fragments attached) from 233 to 541, and

Exhibit 3.1. Design of Teacher-Student and Peer
Collaboration News-Writing Tasks

Writing Sessions	1	2	3	4	5	6	7	8	9
Group 1 (N = 8)	I	I	T	T	I	P	P	I	I
Group 2 (N = 8)	I	I	P	P	I	T	T	I	I

I = Individual Writing Sessions, T = Teacher-Student Collaborations, and P = Peer Collaborations

Writing Prompts (assigned in random order across children)

Renaissance Tasks
Imagine that you are a chronicler living in Italy in 1438. A patron of the Medici family
has hired you to report on an important event:
    Merchants meet to discuss what to do about the city garbage and smells.
Try to use the words *trash* and *aroma*. In your report, (1) write about the event and
(2) tell why the event was important.
(Three similar topics set in the Renaissance were also used.)

Current Tasks
The editor of the Open School newspaper has hired you to report on an important
event:
    *Third and fourth graders from the Open School go on a field trip to the Gardner
Museum.*
Try to use the words *explore* and *artist*. In your report, (1) write about the event and
(2) tell why the event was important.
(Four similar current topics were also used.)

in words from 395 to 2,169. All codes emerged from the data after extensive
and repeated perusal by five raters (interrater reliability was approximately
.75). The codes are as descriptive as possible, rather than evaluative.

One goal of this study was to describe children's approaches to challenging literacy tasks, with peers and a teacher and in contrast to the approach of
the teacher. We focused on two aspects of the participants' approaches to the
writing tasks: the topics of their talk and their verbal interaction styles. To
gain information about the topics that the teacher and children covered and
their diverse interaction styles, we developed two strands of codes: *topic focus*
and *social structure of interaction*. Since we wanted to be sensitive to diversity
across children, we accounted for all topics and social interaction types that
occurred in the data, yielding thirty-two topic focus codes and twenty-eight
social structure codes. In some of the data presented here, codes that were
very low frequency have been eliminated. The children and teacher focused
on a wide range of topics during their collaborative composing sessions, including characters, events, settings, and story significance; rhetorical and
structural features (organization, opening sentences, and paragraphs); composing processes (mention of processes, strategies, and planning); task, style,
mechanics (spelling, capitalization, and punctuation); vocabulary; proce-
dures; personal issues; and off-task talk. The topics on which the participants
chose to focus in their discourse constituted what we referred to as the *cur-*

ricula of the interactions. Identifying such literacy curricula as they emerge in diverse collaborations offers insights about collaboration as an instructional context designed by the participants in that context. While a teacher may tailor discussion topics to her assessments of her students' needs, the children's curricula reflect the aspects of literacy that they feel the need to explore. In fact, we found in previous research that such curricula developed spontaneously by children during collaborative composing with peers included aspects of literacy that were particularly challenging (Daiute, 1989). Identifying these curricula is one way we link the teacher's enculturation of children to literate discourse and children's unique ways of making sense of intellectual problems.

The other strand of codes, social interactions, included asking questions, mentioning a topic or text sequence for the first time (initiating), and repeating a partner's suggestion, disagreeing, agreeing, posing alternatives, evaluating (positively and negatively), expressing internal states and affect, playing, directing, instructing, and elaborating. Identification of the nature of social interactions offers a window into the strategies that children use when approaching literacy tasks. The topic focus and social structure codes were entered into the transcripts using the CHILDES language analysis system (MacWhinney and Snow, 1990), which was then used for computations.

We explored and qualitatively described differences between the teacher's interactions and children's interactions with the teacher and with a peer using two types of statistical analyses. Repeated-measures analysis of variance (ANOVA) was used to assess differences in the mean frequencies of individual codes across interactions. Principal components analysis (PCA) was used to explore relationships among talk and text variables within and across groups and to help us identify patterns among variables. This analysis examined intercorrelated variables and created composite variables for the groups and for each participant.

Text Analyses. This study was based on the idea that social interaction engages children in more complex composing strategies than they use on their own at this age, with the dialogic nature of collaborative composing involving children in extended deliberations about ideas and text. As it turned out, the children focused intensely on a wide range of text features to an extent that would probably not have occurred without such collaborative experiences. Since the narrative task was held constant over time, we identified narrative text features; and since we thought that social interaction might engage children in playing with and crafting texts as they would other physical and intellectual objects, we analyzed text features that characterize written rather than oral language. Based on extensive comparisons of oral and written language, researchers have identified syntactic, lexical, and other features that characterize standard written English, including the use of complex noun phrases, prenominal modifiers, third-person references, and complex sentences (Chafe and Danielewicz, 1987).

Our hypothesis was that in the context of social interaction children treat their texts more as crafted objects than they had before deliberating, examining, and constructing texts with a partner and with different partners—the teacher and a peer. The written features analysis seemed especially interesting to use because playing with a text, as children tend to do when working with their peers, might allow children to manipulate written language with increasing facility. In addition, the more freedom children have to use their familiar oral language as they shape written language, the easier it may be for them to use the written genre required in school. By linking changes in the written features of children's individual texts to processes of teacher-student and peer collaboration, we were able to explore relationships between diverse discourse patterns and the shaping of texts.

Since the task in this study was to write a news story, we also did a story elements analysis, which involved documenting the presence of settings, characters, events, problems, evaluations (see Daiute and Griffin, this volume), resolutions, dialogue, and other rhetorical devices (such as first-person narrator) in the text (Daiute and Dalton, 1993; Zajac, 1992). In addition to noting the story elements occurring in each text, the analysis indicates the elaborations on each element, such as describing a character rather than only introducing a character. The number of words in each text was computed, because for children at this age production is an important feature (Applebee, Langer, Mullis, and Jenkins, 1990; Daiute, 1989; Snow and others, 1991). Once the variables offering the most descriptive information were identified, the following list of text variables was used in subsequent analyses: number of words per text, number of complex noun phrases, number of prenominal modifiers, frequency of third-person references, total story elements, total number of elaborations of story elements, number of evaluations, and character-focused evaluations.

Literacy Curriculum as It Evolves in Socially Mediated Writing Activities

The teacher and children focused on a wide range of literacy and literacy-related topics during their collaborative composing sessions, but the relative frequencies of utterances differed among the children when they worked with the teacher versus when they worked with a peer, as well as between the teacher and the children.

Table 3.1 lists the mean frequencies of utterances focusing on each topic that emerged during collaborative composing sessions by children writing with peers and with the teacher. In interpreting these differences in means, it is important to consider that, on average, the teacher spoke 1,902 words in collaboration sessions, while children spoke 865 words on average when collaborating with peers, and 572 words on average when collaborating with the teacher. Although the teacher spoke two to three times as much as the children in different situations, the children had more utterances focused on certain topics, while the teacher focused more often on other topics. All of the participants talked at least once about all of the topics that emerged, even though frequencies varied across participants and situations.

As shown in Table 3.1, the teacher spoke more about all topics except importance of event, spelling, and capitalization. Remarkably, any differences between how much the children and the teacher talked about the significance of story events, endings, text length, titles, and target words did not

Table 3.1. Mean Frequency of Talk Around Literacy Features
by Teacher, Children with Teacher, and Children with Peers
During Collaborative Composing

	Teacher (N = 32[a])		Child with Teacher (N = 32[a])		Child with Peer (N = 16[a])	
	Mean	SD	Mean	SD	Mean	SD
Narrative Features						
Character	54.6	18.7	30.3	15.3	33.4	16.9
Event	73.9	20.2	41.7	20.1	33.4	17
Orientation	5.1	3.5	2.4	2.4	6.2	5.1
Explanation	2.3	2.7	1.3	1.4	2.3	3.8
Importance of event	0.3	.6	0.4	.7	0.3	.5
Description	1.4	1.9	0.2	.4	0.0	.1
Content	30.6	13.0	10.1	4.0	5.9	2.6
Structure						
Opening sentences	1.0	1.1	0.3	.6	0.1	.2
Ending	0.9	1.0	0.3	.5	0.4	1.3
Organization	4.0	2.7	0.4	1.1	0.3	.3
Length	0.4	.7	0.3	.6	0.4	.7
Paragraph	0.6	.8	0.1	.3	0.1	.1
Title	0.6	1.7	0.6	1.9	0.0	0.0
Task						
Task	3.5	1.9	0.4	0.6	2.1	1.7
Target words	6.0	4.0	3.4	2.4	3.7	3.4
Mechanics						
Spelling	11.0	5.1	8.2	5.3	25.7	17.1
Punctuation	1.1	1.8	0.2	0.4	0.7	0.5
Capitalization	0.5	0.7	0.2	0.4	0.6	0.9
Style	7.4	4.0	1.3	1.2	0.9	1.4
Process						
Composing process	31.6	12.6	4.1	2.5	12.7	5.6
Procedures	6.7	3.4	2.2	2.1	6.5	3.2

[a] N = Number of composing sessions and transcripts.

occur at greater than chance levels. Thus, children developed for themselves a challenging curriculum.

Patterns of Talk

In the ongoing flow of composing, the teacher and children addressed myriad topics, as illustrated in Table 3.1 and discussed above. The PCA suggested that through their discourse the teacher and children chose diverse approaches to the same set of writing tasks.

Teacher's Curriculum. The teacher's curriculum is characterized by four different patterns of talk: *narrative/strategy focus, content focus, structure focus,* and *text form focus.* The teacher's narrative/strategy orientation involves discussing several narrative elements (characters, events, descriptions, and significances of events) and several cognitive strategies (planning and deliberations of style) (see Daiute and others, 1993, for details of the PCAs). This narrative/strategy focus accounts for a relatively large number of her interactions, but the teacher tended to focus in this way with some children more than with others. For example, in the following excerpt of talk, the teacher used the narrative/strategy focus with Rebecca.

1 TEACHER: Okay, maybe, as guests, as the guests leave the great hall they enter the garden where there's a beautiful fountain.
2 REBECCA: Right, there's a beautiful fountain with . . .
3 TEACHER: Okay. Let's see, then we can go, what'd I say, as the . . .
4 REBECCA: As the guests leave the [sigh] the great hall.
5 TEACHER: Oof, I keep doing that all day, the, the, the . . .
6 REBECCA: The great . . .
7 TEACHER: Hall.
8 REBECCA: They walk into the garden. A frog spitting water into a fountain.
9 TEACHER: [Laughs] To the and instantly # and see a beautiful sculpture.
10 REBECCA: And see a beautiful sculpture of a spitting frog.
11 TEACHER: [Laughs]
12 REBECCA: That's how some of them are.
13 TEACHER: [Simultaneously] I know. A beautiful +/ how 'bout a beautifully carved fish, frog, what?
14 REBECCA: Frog.
15 TEACHER: Spitting [laughs].
16 REBECCA: [Laughs] Spitting in towards the water.
17 TEACHER: Spitting water.
18 REBECCA: Into the fountain.
19 TEACHER: How 'bout a beautifully carved fountain of a frog?
20 REBECCA: Yeah. Carved (?) frog +/ spitting water.
21 TEACHER: A frog spitting water.

22 REBECCA: And the frog put his head up and spit at a person.
23 TEACHER: No.
24 REBECCA: [Laughs]
25 TEACHER: Spitting water. Okay. How 'bout the, now let's describe the garden a little.
26 REBECCA: The people were astonished or something.
27 TEACHER: Okay. Let's start with how the garden looked. The courtyard was filled. The garden was . . .
28 REBECCA: With flowers and nice trimmed grass or something.
29 TEACHER: How 'bout filled with sculpture?
30 REBECCA: Sculptures of . . .
31 TEACHER: Statues, how 'bout statues?
32 REBECCA: Statues of famous people or of maybe could be some of the gods or +/
33 TEACHER: We could say statues of the gods, that's a good idea.
34 REBECCA: Of the Greek gods.
35 TEACHER: Of the Greek gods. Good idea.
36 REBECCA: There were nice flowers.
37 REBECCA: Hanging around (?).
38 TEACHER: How 'bout, and spectacular flowers?
39 REBECCA: In my house, my floor and we're getting a paint job.
40 REBECCA: And the floor is getting sanded at my house.
41 TEACHER: Oh, so you're gonna have spectacular floors and gorgeous walls. And plants. What else?

The teacher prompts Rebecca for events (for example, utterance 1) and description related to the setting (for example, utterance 13) and secondary characters. Issues of wording and style also are raised (for example, utterances 30 and 31). In contrast, in her collaboration with Gary, the teacher prompts to review content related to their topic, the significance of events, the importance of having a catchy opening sentence (see earlier-cited excerpt), and so on. Other episodes in the teacher's interactions with Rebecca, Gary, and other children more characteristically include the pattern of variables that combine to make up structure focus and text form focus. The teacher's structure focus involved considerable attention to establishing a time frame for the story, paragraph structure, mechanics, descriptions, and task structure. The teacher tended to focus her conversations in this way with a few children who happened to be among the lowest scorers on standardized texts. It is noteworthy that the teacher focused on structural aspects of texts, like using paragraphs, with children whose individual writing appeared to lack expository structure, such as Shara, whose writing tended to be lengthy and to include overlapping topics. In contrast to the structure focus, the teacher's focus on text form involved a broad range of textual concerns, including style, paragraph, openings, and content.

In summary, the four most recurrent patterns of teacher talk that emerged reflect this teacher's tendency to guide students in focusing on expert composing strategies and aspects of literacy that are typically considered to be problematic for beginning writers, including developing content for a piece of writing, using a prescribed organizational structure, and maintaining consistent use of standard written English forms. The patterns of children's talk with peers revealed a different set of concerns.

Children's Curricula. It is not surprising that when writing with the teacher, the children were influenced by the teacher's guidance on issues of strategy, structure, and style. Nevertheless, the children's topic focus composites when working with the teacher did not exactly parallel the teacher's foci.

Since the primary goal of this study was to understand children's spontaneous approaches to challenging literacy tasks, the curricula that the children created as they composed were of central interest in our analyses. Four topic focus composites emerged from the peer interactions, including children's concerns for a broad range of factors, contextual factors, narrative textures, and personal extensions.

Four talk patterns that characterize the children's interactions when writing with peers are *broad range focus, context focus, narrative focus,* and *personalized narrative focus*. What is remarkable about the children's peer interactions as characterized in the broad range focus is that even though children tended to focus on mechanics (spelling, punctuation, capitalization), which some researchers and teachers say should not be the focus of higher-level tasks like writing, the children also paid attention to narrative elements (character, events, significance of events), structural features of the task and text, content, and composing processes. This broad range focus by even the lowest-achieving writers in the group when working with peers shows that children can attend to many aspects of a complex task like writing. The peers' context focus involved discussing a range of factors that frame the text and task, including time setting, task requirements, and relationships between historical topics and their personal lives. The peers' narrative focus involved an intense orientation to narrative features, including significance of the story, characters, descriptions, events, and mechanics. The personalized narrative focus involved attention to narrative features, with interpretation of these features in terms of personal concerns.

Across these topic focus patterns by the children writing with peers, we observed a general penchant among the children to use collaborative discourse to link text to broader contexts of the task and their personal lives, in contrast to the teacher's tendency to help children address the types of structural issues that present problems for many children in school-based literacy assessments. This contrast is reflected in the earlier cited dialogue excerpts, which show the teacher engaging her students in thinking about the text from a structural point of view, and in the following excerpt by Lisa and Kay, which is a characteristic example of children drawing on social and emotional resources to make sense of a school experience and their writing task (see Daiute and Griffin, this volume, for a more detailed discussion of this contrast).

LISA: Okay, does this sound good? When we went to the th // third floor, we wanted to know if we could go up to the fourth floor.

KAY: They said we couldn't because that's where Elisabel, Isabella, was # like, that's where Isabella lived.

LISA: Okay, that's great. And then we would say, then we could say, we couldn't cuz that's where . . .

KAY: Isabella lay // lived. That's her bedroom.

LISA: [Simultaneously] And that's where she lay, she lays.

KAY: She did?

LISA: No.

KAY: They buried her there?

LISA: I think so . . .

KAY: No, I think.

LISA: NO, they didn't!!!!

KAY: No I think, I think.

LISA: They didn't bury her, cuz who would want her to be in a . . .

KAY: Museum.

LISA: A museum, cuz then her body would like . . .

KAY: Rot?

LISA: Yeah # okay.

KAY: So, yeah . . .

LISA: I know, she would turn to aaa [cough].

KAY: (?) # so they said.

LISA: She would sorta like form into the way she would like be, turned into ashes or something.

KAY: [Anxious giggle]

LISA: I know. Did you know that when we went there, when I was on the third floor, it gave me the creeps, cuz of those stairways. And it was dark sometimes and then light?

KAY: Lisette, Lisette, can I write now?

Nature of Social Interaction Around Challenging Writing Activities

Table 3.2 lists the mean frequencies of social structure talk of various kinds during collaborative composing by the teacher, children with the teacher, and children with peers. As shown in this table, the speech of the teacher and of the children served a broad range of social functions. There were, however, striking differences between the teacher's talk and children's talk when they worked with the teacher or with a peer. More of the teacher's utterances were independent and exerted greater cognitive control over the interaction. The teacher engaged in more eliciting, instructing, initiating, and posing of alternatives. In contrast, more of the children's utterances were interdependent and affectively charged, including playing, disagreeing, and making personal connections.

The PCA revealed three interactional styles characteristic of the teacher, which she applied differently across children. This teacher guided her students closely during their collaborations, as reflected in the *teacher control* pattern, including instructing, repeating, directing, disagreeing, elaborating, answering, indirect directing, and affirming. Although a few of the variables in this pattern reflect mutuality (answering and affirming), this composite indicates a relatively unilateral style. The *direct feedback* composite revealed this teacher's tendency to let children know when they are and are not conforming to her plan—an approach that has been debated in recent literacy research. Although the teacher provided feedback by affirming, evaluating negatively, and directing, some of her direction is couched as collaborative, as in "Let's do a good opening sentence," even though it functions as a command. The interactional pattern, *responsive teacher*, was, in contrast, collaborative in that the teacher was responding to a relatively large number of her young partner's questions, directing in a collaborative way, and building on her partner's suggestions of text sequences. As discussed below, this pattern is most similar to the peers' interactional styles, and it is the teacher's pattern that most strongly relates to positive changes in her partner's writing.

The children's interactional styles differed considerably from the teacher's. Parallel with the broad range topic focus pattern, the peers tended to use a wide range of social interactions as well, as reflected in the *wide range* composite, including asking questions, monitoring, directing, answering, initiating, repeating, disagreeing, negatively evaluating, and playing. Another frequently occurring pattern of the children was highly *affective* talk, involving use of affect verbs, playing, asking questions, negative evaluating, directing, disagreeing, and positive evaluating. Both the wide range and affective patterns accounted for a considerable amount of the variance among children. A third pattern evidenced by some of the children was *intense engagement* during these writing activities, including positive evaluating, initiating, elaborating, asking questions, playing, and negative evaluating. The excerpt of conversation between Lisa and Kay and the excerpt from Andy and Russ illustrate these characteristic interaction patterns in different ways. For example, both excerpts reflect affective orientations; Lisa and Kay refer directly to their feelings, and Andy and Russ play with ideas.

The differences in interactional styles of the teacher and of the children when working with peers isolate a few aspects of socially mediated literacy that may be key to understanding the circumstances of literacy development and learning. Just as the teacher's and children's curricula differed in terms of their relative focus on structure and sense, the interactional patterns differed

Table 3.2. Mean Frequency of Social Structure Talk by
Teacher, Children with Teacher, and Children with Peers
During Collaborative Composing

Social Structure Talk	Teacher (N = 32[a])		Child with Teacher (N = 32[a])		Child with Peer (N = 16[a])	
	Mean	SD	Mean	SD	Mean	SD
Words spoken	1901.8	347.4	571.8	190.4	865.0	306.6
Asking questions	68.7	16.2	15.2	7.6	24.3	8.6
Planning	39.3	14.2	3.4	3.1	7.6	5.6
Initiating text sequences	32.6	8.5	14.8	5.2	11.9	4.2
Initiating when requested	0.6	0.6	5.3	3.3	0.3	0.4
Instructing	23.6	10.8	1.8	2.2	5.7	3.3
Posing alternatives	21.8	4.6	7.4	3.3	10.0	6.7
Evaluating, positively	8.7	2.7	1.2	1.5	2.5	2.0
Evaluating, negatively	2.0	1.7	0.5	0.6	4.0	5.
Disagreeing	3.2	2.5	2.3	2.1	10.9	8.5
Playing	4.7	4.3	2.3	2.7	22.7	25.6
Directing	16.8	7.1	1.4	1.2	21.2	12.3
Indirect directing	15.7	5.6	0.7	1.0	2.3	2.0
Repeating	23.6	10.9	21.2	11.8	19.7	7.1
Personal connections	2.4	2.0	2.6	3.6	10.4	19.8
Emotion words in text sequences	2.7	3.4	1.2	1.2	1.4	2.1
Affect in discussion	7.9	3.9	1.1	1.4	3.5	3.6
Text production	32.3	8.7	36.2	15.0	35.9	19.1

[a] N = Number of composing sessions and transcripts.

in terms of the extent to which the participant drew on social and affective resources versus individual and cognitive resources. These issues of control and mutuality have been discussed by educators and researchers in relation to teaching, learning, and development throughout this century. Issues of cognitive versus affective orientation, however, have not been seen as related to social interaction or intellectual development. The occurrence of such diverse approaches to working collaboratively around text suggests that we need more detailed theories about the nature and value of collaboration. Children's high reliance on affective resources relative to the teacher suggests that our models of literacy need to better account for this orientation. Our data offer insights about what different collaborative situations provide and which aspects favor positive changes in writing. These results further support increased consideration to affective orientations.

Nature of Changes in Children's Individual Writing Before and After Collaboration

The design of this study allowed us to compare changes in the written features of children's individual texts before and after composing with the teacher twice and with a peer twice. Changes in children's use of third-person references, complex noun phrases, prenominal modifiers, and so on, adjusted for the number of words written, were considered in a PCA to determine patterns of change in writing after collaborating with the teacher or a peer. This PCA on written feature change scores yielded four composites: two patterns of complexity in written features after working with the teacher and two patterns of complexity in written features after working with a peer. Each child was given a standardized profile of changes in individual writing. This analysis showed that some children wrote in a more writerly style, that is, more written features, after collaborating with the teacher. A different group of children wrote with more written features after collaborating with a peer. And a third group increased the number of written features of their texts after collaborating both with the teacher and with a peer.

Two patterns of change occurred after children collaborated with the teacher. The *elaborated classic narrative structure* composite was composed of children's increased text length, elaboration of narrative elements (like character and event descriptions), use of complex noun phrases, use of prenominal modifiers, use of third-person references, and use of narrative element types. The other composite for post–teacher collaboration writing complexity is the *classic* composite, which is characterized by changes in use of third-person references and total narrative elements but not by increases in text length or elaborations of narrative elements. The writing of four children changed in either one or both of these patterns after working with the teacher. Seven children changed in one or both of these patterns *and* in different ways that characterized post–peer collaboration writing.

Two patterns of change occurred in the literary nature of children's individual writing after they composed with peers. The *fluent/decentered* composite emphasized elaborations in narrative elements but not changes in the total number of narrative elements. The other composite, *toward classic*, involved a shift toward third-person references and increased text length but not a change in use of prenominal modifiers or complex noun phrases.

The following samples of written narratives illustrate these changes in the writing of two students: Rebecca, whose writing scored high on the elaborated classic composite and classic composite for post–teacher collaboration changes, and Lisa, whose writing scored high on the fluent/decentered composite and toward classic composite for post–peer collaboration changes.

Rebecca's Writing Before Collaborating with the Teacher

The thierd and fourth graders from 302 went to the Gardner Museum and saw some Land scapes, Portrets, The wheel of fourtune and learned about all different things. They saw the court yard, statchues and Tapestrees. I bet they had alot of fun.

Rebecca's Writing After Collaborating with the Teacher

there is a cathedral for Saint Marry of the Flower, and now Filippo needs to build a Dome alot of people have ideas on how to do it. But Filippo thought he could do it with out a saport. All the people laughed at him. Filippo got mad and started to yell. The gaurds took Filippo away. The people had a contest to see hoo could make an egg stand up the winner would get to build the Dome. Filippo went to the countest and won because he just smushed the egg on the bottom and it stood. So Filippo got to build the Dome. He died before he finished the Dome but his friends finished it for him.

Lisa's Writing Before Collaborating with a Peer

I played the recorder for the "Renaissance Fair". The word Renaissance means rebirth. In the "Renaissance Fair Sue played a song on the recorder & Ian juggled. Evan played a song on the recorder & after he played the song we had a feast. I play the piano & I play the recorder. I like to play the piano & I like to play the recorder. I like to play alot of instruments & when we had the "Renaissance Fair we had a celebration!

Lisa's Writing After Collaborating with a Peer
FILIPPO'S DOME!

There are alot of archects in the whole world. But in the "Renaissance" like these people & they are: Donetello, Laonardo, Michelangelo, Rapiel, Ghiberti & Filippo. One day the judes thought Filippo couldn't finish the dome by his self so they let Ghiberti help Filippo finish the dome. But the judes didn't know that Ghiberti didn't know what Filippo was doing. Filippo knew Ghiberti would be helping so Filippo pretended he was sick and when the judes came back to the dome it wasn't finished. And the judes said "Hey you didn't do anything and Ghiberti said "I didn't know what to do. And then Filippo was all better & filippo finished the dome all by his self. And the judes said hey what do know Filippo did finish the dome & they never did that again to Filippo all the time he was alive. HE FINISHED THE DOME!

The writing of five children changed in one or both of the post–peer collaboration patterns, whereas their writing had not changed positively after collaboration with the teacher. Thus, collaboration with the teacher and a peer related to increases in the written features of narrative writing for most of the children, but some children took more away from writing with the teacher, and others from writing with a peer. Moreover, the nature of the changes after each situation differed.

One of the important differences between the postteacher and postpeer narrative texts was the number of total narrative elements. This variable captures children's expansion of their narrative frame to include a new feature like setting, problem, or resolution. Although we observed changes in story frames among peers of the same age in previous research (Daiute and Dalton, 1993), the children in the present study had more extensive narrative-writing experiences and thus most of them wrote stories with at least the basic elements of character, setting, and plot. Thus, expansion of one's story frame in the present study was probably a more difficult achievement. The teacher's emphasis on moving on in the story, writing the next part, engaged children in the writing of stories with more elaborate story frames when they composed with her, and some of the children seemed to extend this frame elaboration to subsequent individual composing sessions.

The relatively small number of children with distinctive cultural, academic, and personal profiles in this study made it difficult to explore whether gender, race, academic ability, or socioeconomic background was correlated with differences in how the teacher interacted with each child or with how children benefited from the various situations. Even with the small number of children observed, however, the results indicate that simple groupings according to race, class, or academic achievement would not account for the patterns of change in individual writing before and after collaboration. Gender proved slightly clearer in terms of differences in teacher-child interaction; but even in this case, where there appears to be a pattern, we cannot say anything conclusive.

Relationships Between Talk and Changes in Children's Individual Writing Over Time

Several of the twenty-four composites of topic focus and social structure of interaction discussed above were significantly correlated at the 1.0 level with components of change in children's individual writing. Considered together, these results suggest that socially mediated literacy activity has an impact on text composing. The teacher talk pattern teacher control correlated negatively with the elaborated classic writing change component, although this statistic just approached significance at the $p < .05$ level ($r = -.44; p = .08$). The teacher's tendency to control the content and form of the text made it unlikely that most of the children would write more elaborated narratives.

Consistent with this finding are correlations between peer interaction components and positive changes in children's writing after composing with peers. Engaging in talk that served a wide range of social functions, from asking questions and initiating text sequences to playing, was positively associated with the change toward writing in the third person ($r = .45; p = .08$). Composing with a peer partner in a highly interactive and committed way was positively correlated with changes toward elaborated narrative texts.

Children's Approaches to Challenging Literacy Activities

The analyses of the curricula and interaction patterns illustrate how children's approaches to literacy tasks differ from those of their teacher. This contrast offers insights into how children make sense of literacy tasks in school.

Several qualities differentiated children's approaches from the teacher's approach, as revealed in the analyses of topic focus and social interaction during collaborative composing. Similar to descriptions of experienced writers and readers, the teacher was goal-directed when she composed with her young partners. This adult's role as teacher as well as collaborator may have involved her in taking different approaches than she would have with a peer collaborator or on her own, but the nature of her composing was strikingly similar to what has been described in the literature on expert composing (Bereiter and Scardamalia, 1987; Collins, Brown, and Newman, 1989; Flower and Hayes, 1981). In particular, as shown in results and examples of the analyses, the teacher was goal-directed. She kept up the pressure to move on to the next aspect of the task—the next part of the narrative—and she focused on strategic aspects of composing such as taking the reader's point of view, writing catchy opening sentences, including vivid descriptions, and composing before revising. In addition, the teacher framed the composing sessions, in part, in terms of the structure of the texts she was creating with her young partners as well as in terms of composing strategies.

In contrast, the children tended to build their composing strategies on social interactions like playful banter, debating, and role playing. These social strategies became composing strategies, since children's interactions tended to stay closely focused on the texts they were creating. In addition, the children's composing was dominated by a search to make sense out of the task and to relate their own personal experiences and feelings to the task. While the teacher was able to keep the task in sharp focus, the children tended to shift fluidly between a sharp focus on the text, as when trying to spell difficult words, and the context, including use of their experiences, understandings, and feelings to make sense of the task.

While the teacher was sometimes playful for the sake of fun, she also seemed to use play as a deliberate strategy to help make a point, to relax a student, or to create solidarity. In contrast, the children's play appeared to be a struggle to impose meaning and familiar strategies on the strange activity of writing reports. The ability to work on a socially meaningful task like creating a newspaper with a peer who understands the world in similar ways and is equal in status helped the children engage their more spontaneous strategies.

Conclusion

This research begins to tease apart specific processes in writing that occur in the context of collaboration. The study showed that expertise is not the most important quality in a collaborator. The teacher, with her expert literacy knowledge and practice, was helpful to some children, but the nature of the interaction around literacy was more important than the absolute expertise of any partner. The teacher's extreme control over ideas and process was negatively associated with the children's ability to benefit from interacting with her. Similarly, children's mutual engagement with ideas, each other, and text when they worked with peers and their coverage of a wide range of text issues were positively associated with text changes. When the children's writing incorporated more features of standard written English after working with the teacher, it was in situations where the teacher was responsive to her partner, in particular by answering the child's questions and by elaborating on specific suggestions for text sequences proposed by the child. Such responsiveness and other forms of effective social interaction were related to the construction of text sequences rather than to positive evaluation or other, more commonly noted features of good teaching. Since peer collaboration of the kind illustrated here, including play, extensive exploration, and reliance on social and affective supports, is not typical school behavior, these results suggest that educators need to rethink the design of instructional contexts.

Note

1. The following transcript codes are used in this chapter: # = pause, +/ = interrupted speech, // = self-correction, (?) = unclear word or words, . . . = trailing off.

References

Applebee, A., Langer, J., Mullis, I., and Jenkins, L. *The Writing Report Card, 1984–1988.* Princeton, N.J.: Educational Testing Service, 1990.

Bereiter, C., and Scardamalia, M. *The Psychology of Written Composition.* Hillsdale, N.J.: Erlbaum, 1987.

Chafe, W., and Danielewicz, J. "Properties of Spoken and Written Language." In R. Horowitz and F. J. Samuels (eds.), *Comprehending Oral and Written Language.* San Diego: Academic Press, 1987.

Collins, A., Brown, J. S., and Newman, S. "Cognitive Apprenticeship: Teaching the Craft of Reading, Writing, and Mathematics." In L. Resnick (ed.), *Knowing, Learning, and Instruction: Essays in Honor of Robert Glaser.* Hillsdale, N.J.: Erlbaum, 1989.

Daiute, C. "Play as Thought: Thinking Strategies of Young Writers." *Harvard Educational Review,* 1989, *59,* 1–23.

Daiute, C., and Dalton, B. " 'Let's Brighten It Up a Bit': Collaboration and Cognition in Writing." In B. Rafoth and D. Rubin (eds.), *The Social Construction of Writing.* Norwood, N.J.: Ablex, 1988.

Daiute, C., and Dalton, B. "Collaboration Between Children Learning to Write: Can Novices Be Masters?" *Cognition and Instruction,* 1993, *10,* 1–43.

Daiute, C., and others. "Young Authors' Interactions with Peers and a Teacher." Unpublished manuscript, Graduate School of Education, Harvard University, 1993.

Dyson, A. H. *Multiple Worlds of Child Writers: Friends Learning to Write.* New York: Teachers College Press, 1989.

Flower, L., and Hayes, J. "The Pregnant Pause: An Inquiry into the Nature of Planning." *Research in the Teaching of English,* 1981, *15* (3), 229–243.

Graves, D. H. *Writing: Teachers and Children at Work.* Portsmouth, N.H.: Heinemann Educational Books, 1983.

MacWhinney, B., and Snow, C. E. "The Child Language Data Exchange System: An Update." *Child Language,* 1990, *17,* 457–472.

Nystrand, M., and Gamoran, A. "Instructional Discourse, Student Engagement, and Literature Achievement." *Research in the Teaching of English,* 1991, *25,* 261–290.

Nystrand, M., Greene, S., and Wiemelt, J. "Where Did Composition Studies Come from? An Intellectual History." *Written Communication*, in press.

Palinocsar, A., and Brown, A. "Reciprocal Teaching of Comprehension and Comprehension Fostering Activities." *Cognition and Instruction*, 1984, *1*, 117–175.

Rogoff, B. *Apprenticeship in Thinking*. New York: Oxford University Press, 1990.

Snow, C. E., and others. *Unfulfilled Expectations: Home and School Influences on Literacy*. Cambridge, Mass.: Harvard University Press, 1991.

Vygotsky, L. S. *Mind in Society: The Development of Higher Psychological Processes*. (M. Cole, V. John-Steiner, S. Scribner, and E. Souberman, eds.) Cambridge, Mass.: Harvard University Press, 1978.

Wood, D., and Middleton, D. "A Study of Assisted Problem-Solving." *British Journal of Psychology*, 1975, *17*, 89–100.

Zajac, R. "Friends and Nonfriends: Collaboration on a Written Text." Unpublished honors thesis for B.A. degree, Institute of Child Development, University of Minnesota, 1992.

COLETTE DAIUTE is associate professor at the Graduate School of Education, Harvard University.

CAROLYN H. CAMPBELL, TERRI M. GRIFFIN, and MAUREEN REDDY are doctoral candidates at the Graduate School of Education, Harvard University.

TERRENCE TIVNAN is a lecturer at the Graduate School of Education, Harvard University.

PART TWO

Literacy Skills in Context

Teachers can enhance their students' vocabularies and provide a foundation for subsequent reading achievement by engaging them in discussions that include low-frequency words.

Learning Vocabulary in Preschool: Social and Discourse Contexts Affecting Vocabulary Growth

David K. Dickinson, Linda Cote, Miriam W. Smith

In this chapter, we discuss social factors that have an impact on children's acquisition of vocabulary in early childhood settings. First, we consider why vocabulary is of great interest to educators. Next, we present a socially contextualized model of word learning. Finally, drawing on data from a longitudinal study of language and literacy development of low-income children, we discuss early childhood classrooms as lexical environments.

Vocabulary Size, Reading Comprehension, and World Knowledge

If one were to select a single variable to measure aspects of children's cognitive functioning related to school success, vocabulary would be a likely candidate because it is closely linked to academic achievement in general and reading comprehension in particular. Data from fifteen countries at three ages (ten, fourteen, and seventeen) reveal correlations between reading comprehension and vocabulary averaging between .66 and .71 (Anderson and Freebody, 1981). The importance of having a large vocabulary is highlighted

The work reported in this chapter is currently supported by Project Head Start and the Spencer Foundation. Previous support was provided by the Ford Foundation. We gratefully acknowledge their support and the efforts of Petra Nicholson, tireless collector of data, and Sarah Gay, transcriber and general helper.

by the research-based estimate that, between grades three and nine, children encounter words from 88,500 word families representing over 100,000 different meanings when reading textbooks written in English (Nagy and Herman, 1987).

The relationship between vocabulary size and reading comprehension cannot be explained simply in terms of readers' failure to understand the meaning of particular words. This explanation has been rejected for two reasons: merely reducing the number of difficult words in passages does not necessarily result in better comprehension, and teaching children new words results in improved comprehension only in certain circumstances (for reviews, see Anderson and Freebody, 1981; Mezynski, 1983; Stahl and Fairbanks, 1986). The currently favored explanation for the link between vocabulary and comprehension is that vocabulary size reflects broad-based and readily retrievable knowledge about the world. Thus, the most successful vocabulary instruction programs now strive to provide children multiple opportunities to develop background knowledge (for example, Beck, McKeown, and Omanson, 1987; Graves, 1987; Pressley, Levin, and McDaniel, 1987).

Vocabulary and Decontextualized Language Skills

Another possible reason for the strong linkage between vocabulary and reading comprehension may be that vocabulary size is a good indicator of decontextualized language skill, that is, discourse-level skill using language to create meanings that can be interpreted apart from the setting in which the language is being used. Examples of decontextualized language include discussions of past and future events, explanations, and analysis of physical or social causality. In each case, language is used to create explicit meanings primarily by means of words and syntax rather than by reliance on gestures and unstated meanings. By the middle of elementary school, children's decontextualized language skills are associated with literacy and school achievement whereas conversational language skill is not similarly related (Snow, Cancino, Gonzalez, and Shriberg, 1989; see Wells, 1986, for a compatible discussion).

Recently, researchers working with the Home-School Study of Language and Literacy Development have found a positive correlation between kindergarten children's story understanding and receptive vocabulary. Furthermore, the same set of experiences seem to foster development of vocabulary and decontextualized language skill. In the home, exposure to explanatory talk during meal times and book reading when children were three and four years old correlate with both sets of language skills (Beals and DeTemple, 1992; Beals, DeTemple, and Dickinson, in press). Similar results emerged from examination of children's preschool experiences: opportunities to engage with teachers in cognitively rich conversations are related to later story understanding and vocabulary (Dickinson and Smith, 1991, 1993). Thus, the relationships between vocabulary, reading comprehension, and discourse-level language skills begin to emerge as early as kindergarten (Dickinson and Snow, 1987).

Learning Words from Context

Estimates of vocabulary size indicate that the average kindergartner knows roughly eight thousand to ten thousand words, and the average high school senior has a vocabulary of roughly forty thousand words (Nagy and Herman, 1987). Such size estimates have led many to conclude that the dominant means by which children acquire new words during the school years is from context as they read (Drum and Konopak, 1987; Nagy, Herman, and Anderson, 1985; Sternberg, 1987). Support for this supposition comes from numerous studies that have found that words first encountered while reading can be learned and recalled over long periods of time (Nagy and Herman, 1987; Jenkins, Stein, and Wysocki, 1984; Wixson, 1986; Herman, Anderson, Pearson, and Nagy, 1987). Of course, given the rapid rate of word learning during early childhood, this ability to learn words from context must emerge during the preschool years. Therefore, if we are to understand how early childhood classrooms support vocabulary growth, we need to understand how children learn words from hearing them.

Words Are Learned Incrementally. We "know" words with varying degrees of completeness, ranging from a vague sense that something is a word to the ability to provide a complete and accurate definition. When children fully know a word, they have at their disposal considerable world knowledge that may include images of multiple exemplars, familiarity with the contexts in which the word is used, and knowledge of event sequences involving exemplars. They also have knowledge about how the word functions in sentences (its syntactic classification, words often used with it), and about semantic relationships to other words (for example, superordinate or subordinate classifications). They have pragmatic information regarding interpersonal and linguistic contexts in which the word might be used (for example, informal versus formal contexts, and genre type). Finally, they are aware of several meanings for the word (for example, *bank* as in "river bank" and "a place with varying interest rates"), and, drawing on their semantic and pragmatic knowledge, they are able to extract those features relevant to a given context when interpreting an utterance. This information is not learned all at once; it is acquired slowly as words are encountered repeatedly in varying contexts and as the concepts that the words map onto become increasingly available (see Rice, 1990; Graves, 1987, for reviews).

Incidental Word Learning. Children begin to learn new words very quickly. After limited exposure to new words, they use linguistic, contextual, and pragmatic information about word meaning to construct knowledge of how a word functions in sentences and of varied aspects of the meaning of the word (Carey, 1978; Dickinson, 1984; Markman and Wachtel, 1988; Rice and Woodsmall, 1988). These initial representations can endure weeks after children hear new words used only once (Carey, 1978; Dickinson, 1984). A roughly similar picture of initial word learning has emerged from studies of incidental word learning resulting from reading (DeVilliers and Pomerantz, 1992; Jenkins, Stein, and Wysocki, 1984; Herman, Anderson, Pearson, and Nagy, 1987).

Variables Affecting Word Learning. There is considerable variability in how quickly children acquire new words. Child language and reading researchers have converged in identifying factors that influence the speed of word learning.

The age of the child is one important factor. Improvement in incidental word learning occurs between the ages of three and five (Rice and Woodsmall, 1988), with further improvement coming between kindergarten and age twelve (Dickinson, 1984). Age also affects what information children are best able to use, with older children being much more able to use information provided by formal definitions (Dickinson, 1984). Also, children differ from one another in their ability to learn new words, with language-disabled children having special problems (Rice, 1990).

Word learning also is conditioned by factors related to exposure: (1) more frequent exposure results in better learning (Drum and Konopak, 1987; Jenkins, Stein, and Wysocki, 1984; Rice, 1990; Sternberg, 1987); (2) learning is best when rich information regarding the word's meaning is provided, especially when the cues are close to the point when the word is encountered (Drum and Konopak, 1987; Rice, 1990; Sternberg, 1987); (3) learning can occur when a number of new words are introduced (Rice and Woodsmall, 1988), although presentation of too many new words at once can depress learning (Sternberg, 1987); (4) learning is best when children are able to comprehend fully the general passage in which the new word is encountered (DeVilliers and Pomerantz, 1992; Drum and Konopak, 1987); and (5) learning is enhanced when the word is encountered repeatedly in roughly similar grammatical contexts with similar meanings (Rice and Woodsmall, 1988).

Word learning also is affected by factors related to the features specific to the word. For example, verbs pose special problems (Rice and Woodsmall, 1988; Smith and Sachs, 1990). Also, the state of the child's world knowledge affects word learning. For example, preschool-age children have difficulty learning names for materials, reflecting possible problems with the concept of material kind (Dickinson, 1988), and high school students are less likely to learn words related to physics concepts (Drum and Konopak, 1987).

Book Reading as a Source for Vocabulary Learning. Given that children are so adept at learning words from incidental contexts, in early childhood settings vocabulary development might be supported by teacher-child discussions as books are read. It is now a well-established fact that there are cor-relations between the amount of book reading in the home, on the one hand, and literacy and varied aspects of language development, on the other (see Goldfield and Snow, 1984; Mason, 1992; Sulzby and Teale, 1991; Mason and Allen, 1986). Studies based in early childhood classrooms are less abundant. What research there is comes from intervention programs that increase the exposure to books and change the nature of interaction that occurs around books. Positive effects have been reported for a project that involves book reading and follow-up activities (Karweit, in press, 1989), and for an ap-proach in which children and an adult coconstruct familiar stories (Valdez-Menchaca and Whitehurst, 1992; Arnold and Whitehurst, in press). Similarly, intervention studies conducted in Israel found strong effects on literacy-related language skills among school-age children resulting from regular oral reading of stories to groups of children (Feitelson, Kita, and Goldstein, 1986; Feitelson, Goldstein, Iraqi, and Share, 1993; Shimron, in press).

Despite this work, many questions remain: What are the long-term ben-efits of specific types of exposure to books in classrooms? Does book reading that occurs naturally in classrooms affect language development? Do conver-sations outside of book reading contexts affect vocabulary growth?

Adult-Child Conversations as Supports for Vocabulary Learning. Mother-child interactional patterns have various important effects on children's language growth (reviewed by Dickinson and McCabe, 1991); but with few exceptions (for example, Putnam, 1992; McCartney, 1984) re-searchers have not attempted to identify effects of teacher-child interaction outside of book reading on language development. Nonetheless, what we know about vocabulary acquisition strongly suggests that one important classroom-related factor that should contribute to vocabulary growth is the variety of new words to which the child is exposed during the day. To test this hypothesis, we developed an approach to measuring vocabulary richness and are striving to determine this factor's relationship to language development.

Home-School Study

Currently, David Dickinson and Catherine Snow are directing a longitudinal study of the home and school factors that support the literacy development of low-income children between the ages of three and nine. As part of that project, we are tracing the emergence of various aspects of literacy-related competence and are attempting to determine the sources of social support for each. Examination of factors affecting vocabulary growth includes study of the lexical richness of classrooms and the impact of book reading on vocabu-lary growth.

Lexical Richness. Data from sixty-five preschool classrooms (thirty-three Head Start and thirty-two private) were examined to determine the lexical richness offered by specific classrooms contexts. We used transcriptions of major activity periods: fifteen minutes of free play, fifteen minutes of large group time, ten minutes each of meal time and small group time, and approximately fifteen minutes of book-reading time. Audiotapes were transcribed in a format that enabled computer-assisted data analysis using the CHILDES system. We were interested in determining how often children in each room heard or used low-frequency words. To achieve this goal, we developed a word list that acted as a filter to screen out common words. The Dale-Chall list of three thousand words known by fourth graders served as the backbone of this list. The filter list was then expanded by adding all forms of base words (for example, adding plurals and past tenses), high-frequency spoken words and slang (for example, tummy, mommy, cubby), all proper names, and all forms of address (for example, honey, miss). This list of nearly eight thousand words was then run against the words in the transcripts, resulting in our list of "rare" or low-frequency vocabulary words.

We compared classroom contexts to determine whether certain contexts were more likely to be conducive to the use of rich and varied vocabulary (book reading, free play, teacher-led small group and large group times, and full group book reading). Using *t* tests, we determined that the setting where rare words were most likely to be encountered was small group time. All other settings were roughly equivalent with the exception of book reading, which showed a low rate of teacher use of rare words when her talk was examined apart from the book-reading text. When the words from the story were included, book reading was comparable to other settings. The superiority of teacher-led small group time echoes previous findings that small group time is conducive to cognitively rich conversations (Dickinson and Smith, 1991, 1993).

We also wanted to determine whether there are relationships between teachers' and children's use of rare vocabulary words and children's outcome measures on some of the measures of language and literacy development that we administered to children at the end of kindergarten. These included a measure of receptive vocabulary (Peabody Picture Vocabulary Test [PPVT]), a test of emergent literacy (which combined measures of letter recognition, phonemic awareness, environmental print knowledge, print concepts, and early writing skills), a measure of story understanding (that is, children's responses to questions posed while being read *The Snowy Day* by a tester), and a measure of children's ability to provide a formal definition for words (for example, a cat is a [copula] kind of animal [superordinate] that scratches furniture [constraining information]). Such formal definitions have been found to be closely linked to general literacy growth, perhaps in part because they reflect the ability to talk about language (Snow, Cancino, Gonzalez, and Shriberg, 1989; Watson, 1989).

We found significant relationships between vocabulary richness during meal time and free-play settings and several of our measures of kindergarten language and literacy development. As shown in Table 4.1, the number of

rare or low-frequency words used during meal times by teachers was correlated with vocabulary growth (PPVT), story understanding, and definitional
quality; vocabulary use by both teachers and children during free play was
related to early literacy.

These findings support two conclusions: Exposure to rare words during
activities in preschool classrooms can enlarge children's vocabularies, and
vocabulary is acquired as part of a broader constellation of language and early
literacy skills. The context specificity of our results also is important. Significant relationships between vocabulary use and early language and literacy
development was found only for free play and meal times, suggesting that
words are most likely to be learned in informal settings. It may be that these
are settings in which children and teachers are "tuned in" to one another's
current interests. When children and teachers are fully engaged, it is more
likely that appropriate concepts will be available for mapping onto the new
words and that adequate contextual information will be supplied to enable
children to grasp the intended word-concept mapping. Additionally, especially during free play, children are apt to be able to use the new words themselves as they engage in a conversation that is geared to their particular
interest. Support for this speculation comes from the finding that free play
was the only setting for which there was a significant correlation between
teachers' and children's use of rare words ($r = .61, p < .001$).

Book Reading. Our analysis of raw frequency of vocabulary usage
showed no effects for book reading on children's vocabulary growth, but
separate analyses that examined the discourse within which vocabulary is
encountered paint a different picture. A study of the book-reading events of
twenty-five classrooms that served the first cohort of children when they
were four revealed that most teachers would pause during the reading to ask
questions of the children, to elicit their personal reactions, or to allow them
to chime in on familiar portions of text. By looking at these opportunities for

Table 4.1. Proportions of Rare Vocabulary at Age Four
Correlated with Outcomes at Age Five

Kindergarten Outcome Measures	Percentage of Rare Words			
	Meal Time		Free Play	
	Teacher	Child	Teacher	Child
PPVT	.43**			
Story understanding	.45**			.41**
Definitions	.41**		.37**	
Early literacy			.34*	.28*

Note: PPVT = Peabody Picture Vocabulary Test.

* $p < .05$

** $p \leq .01$

child engagement, we found that particular types of interaction enhance later language and literacy performance.

We were especially interested in interactions that required children to move beyond the text in their responses. The interactions that typified this kind of talk required the child to analyze characters' personality traits and motivations, to speculate about causes for behavior or incidents, to predict upcoming events, and to directly discuss vocabulary. The following example illustrates a teacher's discussion of vocabulary.

TEACHER: What's "the mother bird's soft down"? Does anyone know what that is?
CHILD: It's laying down.
TEACHER: Well, it's not laying down. They call it "against her down." The down are her feathers, her soft feathers.
CHILD: Cuddle, cuddle.
TEACHER: They cuddle against her down, the down is her feathers.

This example demonstrates the teacher's willingness and children's ability to analyze texts in a sophisticated manner that moves beyond the immediate context of the book and the book-reading event. During both school visits, teachers tended to make more such comments than children, not surprising given the greater amount of talk by teachers in these classrooms. However, when analyzed relative to the total number of comments made by conversant (children, teacher), children made a higher proportion of more nonimmediate comments than did teachers. These comments were both spontaneous and prompted by the teachers, pointing to the interactional nature of the event. There is an age-related change, with teachers making more comments that moved beyond the immediate present with the older children ($p < .05$; Dickinson, DeTemple, Hirschler, and Smith, 1992). This result suggests that teachers are sensitive to children's developing verbal and cognitive sophistication.

To determine relationships between school book reading and later performance, we treated the data collected during school visits at ages three and four as predictors, and the tests and tasks given to our target children at age five as outcomes. Using multiple-regression analyses, we built models for predicting performance on the PPVT and the story comprehension task. In an effort to control for potential effects of good teachers that would override the effects of specific interactions during book-reading sessions, we began our analyses with base models that included variables from the teacher interviews and school visits known to be correlated with the outcomes measures (see Dickinson and Smith, in press). For children's vocabulary development, the amount of analytical talk during book reading provided a significant increment to the predictive power of the base model ($R^2 = .56, p < .0001$). For the story comprehension task, the amount of analytical talk during book reading accounted for significant variation in the children's performance ($R^2 = .20, p = .019$).

In summary, our analyses of both vocabulary frequency and book-reading discourse revealed that preschool classrooms contribute to vocabulary growth and that acquisition of the lexicon is connected to broader language and literacy development. Furthermore, we found that the interactive context within which language is used is of critical importance: Exchanges in which teachers and children are actively engaged with each other in intellectually challenging discussions are those that foster the greatest language growth.

Conclusion

Vocabulary size long has been known to be related to literacy and to be affected by social factors, but evidence linking vocabulary growth to specific features of preschool classrooms has been lacking. Our analyses demonstrate that ordinary teachers working in classrooms that serve low-income children can enhance their children's vocabularies by actively engaging them in discussions that include low-frequency vocabulary items. Furthermore, we found that, as early as kindergarten, vocabulary is related to discourse-level language skills, and that this cluster of skills is linked to a variety of measures of emergent literacy.

Increasingly, our schools are populated by children from less economically advantaged backgrounds, by children representing various ethnic and linguistic minority groups, and by children whose first language is not English (Barringer, 1993). For many reasons (such as lower literacy levels, poorer schooling, and limited exposure to English), children from these groups typically have smaller vocabularies than children from white middle- and upper-class homes, a gap that increases with age (Corson, 1983). Given this difference and the fact that increasing numbers of children are attending preschool (Alsalam, Ogle, Rogers, and Smith, 1992, p. 17), it is vital that we find ways to bolster children's language skills during the early childhood period. (See Dickinson [1991, in press] for development of a framework for describing preschool language environments and for suggestions regarding promising approaches to fostering oral language in early childhood settings.) Given that preschools are places where children and teachers have many opportunities for conversations, and that the typical preschool day is not loaded with pressing curriculum objectives, they are settings where facilitation of vocabulary growth is likely to occur and where it could become a priority without requiring major alterations in traditional classroom practices.

References

Alsalam, N., Ogle, L. T., Rogers, G. T., and Smith, T. M. *The Condition of Education: 1992.* Washington, D.C.: U.S. Government Printing Office, 1992.

Anderson, R. C., and Freebody, P. "Vocabulary Knowledge." In J. T. Guthrie (ed.), *Comprehension and Teaching: Research Reviews*. Newark, Del.: International Reading Association, 1981.

Arnold, D. S., and Whitehurst, G. J. "Accelerating Language Development Through Picture Book Reading: A Summary of Dialogic Reading and Its Effects." In D. K. Dickinson (ed.), *Bridges to Literacy: Approaches to Supporting Child and Family Literacy*. Cambridge, Mass.: Blackwell, in press.

Barringer, F. "For Thirty-Two Million Americans, English Is a Second Language." *New York Times*, Apr. 28, 1993, p. A18.

Beals, D., and DeTemple, J. M. "Home Contributions to Early Language and Literacy Development." Paper presented at the annual meeting of the National Reading Association, San Antonio, Texas, Dec. 1992.

Beals, D., DeTemple, J. M., and Dickinson, D. K. "Talking and Listening That Support Early Literacy Development of Low-Income Children." In D. K. Dickinson (ed.), *Bridges to Literacy: Approaches to Supporting Child and Family Literacy Development*. Cambridge, Mass.: Blackwell, in press.

Beck, I. L., McKeown, M. G., and Omanson, R. C. "The Effects and Uses of Diverse Vocabulary Instructional Techniques." In M. G. McKeown and M. E. Curtis (eds.), *The Nature of Vocabulary Acquisition*. Hillsdale, N.J.: Erlbaum, 1987.

Carey, S. "The Child as Word Learner." In M. Halle, G. Miller, and J. Bresnan (eds.), *Linguistic Theory and Psychological Reality*. Cambridge, Mass.: MIT Press, 1978.

Corson, D. "Social Dialect, the Semantic Barrier, and Access to Curricular Knowledge." *Language and Society*, 1983, *12*, 213–222.

DeVilliers, P. A., and Pomerantz, S. B. "Hearing-Impaired Students Learning New Words from Written Context." *Applied Psycholinguistics*, 1992, *13*, 409–431.

Dickinson, D. K. "First Impressions: Children's Knowledge of Words Gained from a Single Exposure." *Applied Psycholinguistics*, 1984, *5*, 359–374.

Dickinson, D. K. "Learning Names for Materials: Factors Constraining and Limiting Hypotheses." *Cognitive Development*, 1988, *3*, 15–36.

Dickinson, D. K. "Teacher Stance and Setting: Constraints on Conversation in Preschools." In A. McCabe and C. Peterson (eds.), *Developing Narrative Structure*. Hillsdale, N.J.: Erlbaum, 1991.

Dickinson, D. K. "Contexts Supporting Oral Language Development in Preschool Classrooms." In J. Duchan (ed.), *Pragmatics: From Theory to Practice*. New York: Praeger, in press.

Dickinson, D. K., DeTemple, J. M., Hirschler, J., and Smith, M. W. "Book Reading with Preschoolers: Co-Construction of Text at Home and at School." *Early Childhood Research Quarterly*, 1992, *7*, 323–346.

Dickinson, D. K., and McCabe, A. "A Social Interactionist Perspective on Language Development." In J. Kavanaugh (ed.), *The Language Continuum*. New York: Praeger, 1991.

Dickinson, D. K., and Smith, M. W. "Preschool Talk: Patterns of Teacher-Child Interaction in Early Childhood Classrooms." *Journal of Research in Childhood Education*, 1991, *6*, 20–29.

Dickinson, D. K., and Smith, M. W. "Contributions of Specific Preschool Experiences to Emerging Literacy Skills." Paper presented at the biennial meeting of the Society for Research in Child Development, New Orleans, Mar. 1993.

Dickinson, D. K., and Smith, M. W. "Long-Term Effects of Preschool Teachers' Book Readings on Low-Income Children's Vocabulary, Story Comprehension, and Print Skills." *Reading Research Quarterly*, in press.

Dickinson, D. K., and Snow, C. E. "Interrelationships Among Prereading and Oral Language Skills in Kindergartners from Two Social Classes." *Early Childhood Research Quarterly*, 1987, *2*, 1–25.

Drum, P. A., and Konopak, B. C. "Learning Word Meanings from Written Context." In M. G. McKeown and M. E. Curtis (eds.), *The Nature of Vocabulary Acquisition*. Hillsdale, N.J.: Erlbaum, 1987.

Feitelson, D., Goldstein, Z., Iraqi, J., and Share, D. L. "Effects of Listening to Story Reading on Aspects of Literacy Acquisition in a Diglossic Situation." *Reading Research Quarterly*, 1993, *28*, 70–79.

Feitelson, D., Kita, B., and Goldstein, Z. "Effects of Listening to Series Stories on First Graders' Comprehension and Use of Language." *Research in the Teaching of English*, 1986, *20*, 339–356.

Goldfield, B. A., and Snow, C. E. "Reading Books with Children: The Mechanics of Parental Influence on Children's Reading Achievement." In J. Flood (ed.), *Understanding Reading Comprehension*. Newark, Del.: International Reading Association, 1984.

Graves, M. F. "The Role of Instruction in Fostering Vocabulary Development." In M. G. McKeown and M. E. Curtis (eds.), *The Nature of Vocabulary Acquisition*. Hillsdale, N.J.: Erlbaum, 1987.

Herman, P. A., Anderson, R. C., Pearson, P. D., and Nagy, W. E. "Incidental Acquisition of Word Meaning from Expositions with Varied Text Features." *Reading Research Quarterly*, 1987, *22*, 263–284.

Jenkins, J. R., Stein, M. L., and Wysocki, K. "Learning Vocabulary Through Reading." *American Educational Research Journal*, 1984, *21*, 767–787.

Karweit, N. "The Effects of a Story-Reading Program on the Vocabulary and Story Comprehension Skills of Disadvantaged Prekindergarten and Kindergarten Students." *Early Education and Development*, 1989, *1*, 105–114.

Karweit, N. "The Effect of Story Reading on the Language Development of Disadvantaged Prekindergarten and Kindergarten Students." In D. K. Dickinson (ed.), *Bridges to Literacy: Approaches to Supporting Child and Family Literacy Development*. Cambridge, Mass.: Blackwell, in press.

McCartney, K. "Effect of Quality of Day Care Environment on Children's Language Development." *Developmental Psychology*, 1984, *20*, 244–260.

Markman, E. M., and Wachtel, G. F. "Children's Use of Mutual Exclusivity to Constrain the Meanings of Words." *Cognitive Psychology*, 1988, *20*, 121–157.

Mason, J. M. "Reading Stories to Preliterate Children." In P. B. Gough, L. C. Ehri, and R. Treiman (eds.), *Reading Acquisition*. Hillsdale, N.J.: Erlbaum, 1992.

Mason, J. M., and Allen, J. "A Review of Emergent Literacy with Implications for Research and Practice in Reading." In C. Z. Rothkopf (ed.), *Review of Research in Education*. Vol. 13. Washington, D.C.: American Educational Research Association, 1986.

Mezynski, K. "Issues Concerning the Acquisition of Knowledge: Effects of Vocabulary Training on Reading Comprehension." *Review of Educational Research*, 1983, *53*, 253–279.

Nagy, W. E., and Herman, P. A. "Breadth and Depth of Vocabulary Knowledge." In M. G. McKeown and M. E. Curtis (eds.), *The Nature of Vocabulary Acquisition*. Hillsdale, N.J.: Erlbaum, 1987.

Nagy, W. E., Herman, P. A., and Anderson, R. C. "Learning Words from Context." *Reading Research Quarterly*, 1985, *20*, 233–253.

Pressley, M., Levin, J. R., and McDaniel, M. A. "Remembering Versus Inferring What a Word Means." In M. G. McKeown and M. E. Curtis (eds.), *The Nature of Vocabulary Acquisition*. Hillsdale, N.J.: Erlbaum, 1987.

Putnam, L. "Inner-City Kindergartners' Vocabulary Development in Three Different Early Literacy Programs." Paper presented at the annual meeting of the National Reading Conference, San Antonio, Texas, Dec. 1992.

Rice, M. L. "Preschoolers' QUIL: Quick Incidental Learning of Words." In G. Conti-Ramsden and C. E. Snow (eds.), *Children's Language*. Vol. 7. Hillsdale, N.J.: Erlbaum, 1990.

Rice, M. L., and Woodsmall, L. "Lessons from Television: Children's Word Learning When Viewing." *Child Development*, 1988, *59*, 420–429.

Shimron, J. "The Making of Readers: The Work of Professor Dina Feitelson." In D. K. Dickinson (ed.), *Bridges to Literacy: Approaches to Supporting Child and Family Literacy Development*. Cambridge, Mass.: Blackwell, in press.

Smith, C. A., and Sachs, J. "Cognition and the Verb Lexicon in Early Lexical Development." *Applied Psycholinguistics*, 1990, *11*, 409–424.

Snow, C. E., Cancino, H., Gonzalez, P., and Shriberg, E. "Giving Formal Definitions: An Oral Language Correlate of School Literacy." In D. Bloome (ed.), *Classrooms and Literacy*. Norwood, N.J.: Ablex, 1989.

Stahl, S., and Fairbanks, M. M. "The Effects of Vocabulary Instruction: A Model-Based Meta-Analysis." *Review of Educational Research,* 1986, *56,* 72–110.

Sternberg, R. J. "Most Vocabulary Is Learned from Context." In M. G. McKeown and M. E. Curtis (eds.), *The Nature of Vocabulary Acquisition.* Hillsdale, N.J.: Erlbaum, 1987.

Sulzby, E., and Teale, W. "Emergent Literacy." In R. Barr, M. L. Kamill, P. Mosenthal, and P. D. Pearson (eds.), *Handbook of Reading Research.* Vol. 2. White Plains, N.Y.: Longman, 1991.

Valdez-Menchaca, M. C., and Whitehurst, G. J. "Accelerating Language Development Through Picture Book Reading: A Systematic Extension to Day-Care." *Developmental Psychology,* 1992, *28,* 1106–1114.

Watson, R. "Literate Discourse and Cognitive Organization: Some Relations Between Parents' Talk and Three-Year-Olds' Thought." *Applied Psycholinguistics,* 1989, *10,* 221–236.

Wells, G. *The Meaning Makers.* Portsmouth, N.H.: Heinemann Educational Books, 1986.

Wixson, K. K. "Vocabulary Instruction and Children's Comprehension of Basal Stories." *Reading Research Quarterly,* 1986, *21,* 317–329.

DAVID K. DICKINSON *is associate professor of education at Clark University, Worcester, Massachusetts.*

LINDA COTE *is a doctoral candidate in the Department of Psychology at Clark University.*

MIRIAM W. SMITH *is a doctoral candidate in the Department of Education at Clark University.*

Children focus on spelling, even in the context of meaningful and social literacy activities and even when they are discouraged from doing so. This chapter discusses children's interest in spelling and illustrates how it can be considered within a social constructionist theory of literacy development.

The Social Construction of Spelling

Maureen Reddy, Colette Daiute

Spelling is not typically a focus of research or practice within a social constructionist theory of literacy. Encoding and decoding are more commonly associated with bottom-up models of reading and writing in which mastery of units like sound-letter correspondences is considered a prerequisite to literacy (Chall, 1983; LaBerge and Samuels, 1974). In more socially oriented theories of literacy (Vygotsky, 1978; Goodman, 1986; Dyson, this volume), the ability to encode sounds into their written forms is secondary to communicative and representational functions. In this chapter, we agree with others who consider literacy a social skill, that purpose, meaning, and symbolic representations are the central issues, but we also argue that the development of these "higher-order" aspects of literacy cannot be considered in isolation from text form. In this view, form follows function, and correct spelling is secondary to having something to say; the ability to spell is the result of a communication history in which a writer employs goals and strategies that have relevance in particular contexts.

In the spelling analysis presented in this chapter, we assume a social constructionist perspective that involves an interplay between the child as a developing speller and the social context in which that development is nurtured. According to the Vygotskian notion that social interaction provides support for children's individual skills (Vygotsky, 1978), spelling can figure in a social constructionist picture in a variety of ways. Children might simply ask for spellings when they have access to another person as a resource. With a reflective teacher or knowledgeable peer, children might also engage in problem solving around spelling that reflects their active involvement with the code of written language. Writers create written words, like ideas and goals, through social interactions around and with specific texts.

Text forms and the systems behind them—like patterned sound-symbol re-lationships—evolve through engagement with text, conversation around text, and internalization of important concepts in the context of a culturally salient task. Thus, such work on spelling may be seen as an analogue to criti-cal text production involving ideas or organization, yet at a level that is both accessible and important to children.

We do not view spelling as an isolated, low-level skill that must be ac-quired before writing, or as a distraction from issues of greater import for composing. Rather, our perspective is that spelling development can be an outcome of writing (and reading) activities and that spelling can be seen as an example of linguistic problem solving, with the possibility that teachers and children make strategies explicit and refine them across time. Furthermore, a collaborative context can provide support for managing the competing de-mands of writing and can offer insights about how to juggle attention to vari-ous skills, ranging from spelling to text organization, for example.

One task facing beginning writers is to figure out the orthographic rules of their language and to relate these to myriad other social and linguistic as-pects of writing. However, little attention has been paid to how children ac-tively acquire skills in context (for exceptions, see Cordeiro, 1988; Wilde, 1988; Scibior, 1987). Consistent with the philosophy of a social construction-ist literacy theory, a major goal of our research is to understand the full range of contextual issues that affect the task of becoming literate. An understand-ing of spelling is important within this larger goal for several reasons. First, written language and its communicative and symbolic functions rely on en-coding, which involves interdependent systems of sound, syntax, semantics, and pragmatics. Given the complexity of the inextricable links across these systems in English, spelling is crucial because beginning writers of all ages find encoding to be a challenge, if not a barrier, to written communication.

Many studies of classroom writing have noted students' concern with and talk about spelling (for example, Blazer, 1986; Daiute and Dalton, 1988; Dyson, 1989; Shaughnessy, 1977). In these studies, spelling has emerged as a concern when students read and write in social contexts, even when spell-ing is not the focus of the teacher, curriculum, or classroom activity. How-ever, spelling has not been the subject of this research. On the other hand, in research specifically about spelling, spelling ability has not been related to the social context of writing; rather, the emphasis has been on the association between spelling and cognitive development (Beers, 1980; Zutell, 1979).

In this chapter, we present a description of third-grade children's talk about spelling as they collaborate on challenging writing tasks. We provide a taxonomy of topics that are of concern to developing spellers as well as com-parisons and contrasts of children of different spelling abilities. We also com-pare the strategies that the teacher uses to help her students spell with the strategies that students use when working together. First, however, we situate our study in relation to two strands of developmental spelling theory and research: spelling stages and spelling strategies.

Developmental Spelling Research

Rather than view nonstandard spellings simply as mistakes, developmental spelling researchers have examined such spellings as evidence of children's theories about written language (Henderson and Beers, 1980; Read, 1971, 1986). Most commonly, children's unconventional spellings are called "invented" (Chomsky, 1971). Invented spelling has garnered renewed interest with the popularity of the process approach to writing (Graves, 1983) and the whole-language movement (Goodman, 1986), both of which advocate more classroom writing and cast the child in the active role of figuring out the system of written English.

Spelling Stages. Interest in children's invented spelling began with Read's (1970, 1971) seminal study of preschoolers. His research showed that children use a rule-governed system to produce spellings that on the surface appear strange. For example, among the many features that he discovered is that children commonly omit the nasals M and N before another consonant, spelling *bump* as B-U-P. Read's insight that such spellings can be seen as a window to children's thinking about written language changed the emphasis in much spelling research from concern about correctness and word difficulty, to interest in spelling as a cognitive and linguistic process.

Although Read does not espouse a stage explanation, his research was inspirational to a large number of studies from which stage theories are derived. In particular, Henderson and his colleagues, in an extensive program of research, concluded that children pass through a series of stages of spelling development (Gentry, 1978; Beers and Henderson, 1977; Henderson, 1980; Ehri, 1992). The idea that children's spelling progress is stagelike has a firm hold on the spelling literature (Buchanan, 1989; Gentry, 1982; McGee and Richgels, 1990). For instance, Gentry (1982; Gentry and Gillet, 1993) delineates five stages of invented spelling: precommunicative, semiphonetic, phonetic, transitional, and conventional. The developmental trend embodied in this framework is for spellers to employ a sequence of strategies: first, using sound, then relying on visual information about orthographic patterns, and, finally, focusing on meaning. Thus, by this account, a child progresses from spelling phonetically to including silent letters that look correct, to considering derivations of words (Henderson and Templeton, 1986).

Such stage theories are derived from children's products. Although some authors (for example, Buchanan, 1989; Gentry and Gillet, 1993) discuss how to ascertain a child's stage from actual compositions, most studies have used prescribed lists of words (see Schlagal, 1989, 1992). Little attention has been paid to the process of spelling. Whereas these stage descriptions appear to be robust findings within the confines of the tasks and populations studied, drawing on the research described in this chapter we argue that a focus on products alone obscures the complexity of what actually occurs when children spell.

Spelling Strategies. Stage theories dominate the spelling literature, yet some whole-language educators discuss the processes of spelling (see Bouffler, 1991; Wilde, 1989, 1992) and advocate that children's strategies be taken into account. For instance, Bouffler (1985) devised the following taxonomy: spelling as it *sounds*, spelling as it *sounds out*, spelling as it *articulates*, spelling as it *means*, spelling as it *looks*, spelling by *analogy*. These categories come largely from observations and interviews rather than analyses of what children say as they compose. In the study described below, we analyzed children's talk about spelling while they were engaged in writing. With this approach, we were able to include a much more extensive description of the spelling processes that the children used when composing.

Furthermore, existing descriptions of spelling processes are not developmental (Wilde, 1992); rather, the strategies are assumed to be used by all spellers, even adults who encounter unfamiliar or difficult words. We looked at cases cross-sectionally to see whether the children in our sample, whose spelling abilities represented a range of achievement, used different spelling processes, and whether the teacher interacted differently with them, adding a developmental viewpoint to existing strategy analyses.

Description of the Study

These data come from a year-long study that took place in an urban third- and fourth-grade classroom (see Daiute, Campbell, Griffin, Reddy, Tivnan, this volume; Daiute and Griffin, this volume). For this study, Ann, a veteran teacher, collaborated with the research team to create writing activities that were consistent with her social studies curriculum, which focused on the Renaissance. From January to June, sixteen children, working on computers, each composed nine stories for publication in the classroom newspaper, *Time Traveler News*. Students completed two writing tasks individually, then wrote twice with a partner, followed by another individual task, then two more collaborative sessions, and finally two individual tasks. Two sequential collaborative sessions were with the teacher and two with a peer. We audiotaped and transcribed all collaborative sessions as data for a study on collaboration. We also collected written products from all nine sessions.

Description of the Spelling Data. Many other analyses concerning the nature of peer and teacher-child collaboration are also being conducted as part of the broader study. The research was not designed as an investigation of spelling per se; rather, spelling emerged as an important concern because the participants often chose to talk about spelling as one aspect of the total writing task. In fact, the topic of spelling (which includes any explicit mention of the word *spelling* or any instances of actual spelling of words) was third most frequent for the children, coming after who and what their stories were about.

In the writing process literature, this kind of interest in spelling is considered problematic because spelling is described as a low-level process that can interfere with higher-level concerns about meaning and organization. Graves (1983, p. 194), for example, claims that "when the mechanics of spelling dominate, when words do not flow from an automatic source, content suffers." In our study, we found evidence that young writers are very interested in spelling while composing, though their teacher adopted the writing process stance of deferring concern about spelling until editing. Our argument is that this interest did not dominate, because it did not interfere with attention to many levels of the writing task. Our coding of topics emerged from the data, and we found that children expressed a broad range of concerns, including such issues as how to organize a piece of writing, what impact their writing would have on an audience, how to put emotion into their compositions, and whether the style fit the message; these are among the many concerns discussed by these young writers, even though they also talked a great deal about spelling.

In using a writing process approach, the teacher told the children to defer concern with spelling until the editing stage. The following remark by Ann to one of her student collaborators exemplifies her policy: "Okay we'll fix it later. Mostly it's important to get the words down." According to Graves (1983), children will be less preoccupied with skills like spelling if teachers emphasize meaning. Indeed, Ann talked frequently about the content of the text, as she did about such concerns as style and organization. Like the children, Ann's most frequent topics were who and what the stories were about; next in frequency was talk about the composing process. She also dealt extensively with issues like vivid description, emotional content, text organization, and style. As with the children, this broad range of topics shows that the teacher was concerned with both meaning and style. Yet, in spite of Ann's admonitions to the contrary, children showed a marked concern about spelling in their talk while composing, especially when they worked with one another and had more control over the conversation. Even when they wrote with Ann, though, they were able to introduce and sustain spelling as a topic of conversation.

We considered the possibility that the amount of spelling talk might be an artifact of the situation in which two people work together on a computer. That is, we wondered if some of the spelling talk consisted of simply verbalizing keystrokes to a partner. We found that this was not the case, since very few (8 percent) of the examples were simply what we termed *production,* that is, spelling aloud without any discussion. Additional instances of production were embedded in conversations about spelling, where, as part of talking about the spelling of a word, the writers named the letters aloud. These instances of production account for 23 percent of the extended talk about spelling.

These data contain information about spelling that is not captured in other studies. For instance, talk about words that were eventually correctly encoded shows the strategies that the children used to come up with conventional spellings. With few exceptions (Scibior, 1987; Wilde, 1992), most ways of evaluating spelling development do not allow for analysis of correctly spelled words because product-based assessments rely only on misspellings.

Furthermore, again with notable exceptions (for example, Downing, DiStephano, Rich, and Bell, 1984; Templeton, 1992; Wilde, 1988), the age range of the children in our study is underrepresented in developmental spelling research, where emphasis is placed on emergent and early literacy. Because of the complexity of the English spelling system (Venezky, 1976), spelling development continues beyond the preschool and primary years. Several researchers have noted that between the second and fifth grades, children's repertoires of spelling strategies expand to include visual factors (Tenney, 1980), consideration of derivational morphology (Templeton, 1980), and use of known-word analogies (Marsh, Friedman, Welch, and Desberg, 1980). Therefore, this description of how third graders grappled with the complexities of the spelling system of English within the context of complicated writing projects may add to our understanding of spelling development in school-age children.

In this chapter, we do not discuss children's misspellings, since the literature is replete with such analyses. We concentrate on what the children and their teacher said about spelling as they worked together. We have taken our cue from the children in our efforts to find ways to study spelling in the context of social interaction.

Categories of Spelling Talk. Given that the children chose to focus a great deal of talk on spelling, what exactly did they talk about? Through inductive analysis of all episodes of talk about spelling, we identified thirty-four different categories of spelling talk: asking the spelling of a whole word, asking the spelling of part of a word, asking confirmation of the spelling of a whole word, asking confirmation of the spelling of part of a word, asking confirmation of a letter, spelling a whole word, spelling part of a word, spelling a letter, confirming the spelling of a whole word, confirming the spelling of part of a word, confirming a letter, talking about knowing (or not knowing) how to spell, negatively evaluating self as speller, negatively evaluating partner, positively evaluating partner, talking about rules or terms, talking about morphemes, producing, jointly producing, talking about an unusual word, sounding out, spelling by syllables, deferring concern about spelling, checking a spelling by sight, checking a spelling by meaning, checking a spelling by reading, checking a spelling by sound, checking a spelling by memory, contesting part of a word, contesting a whole word, contesting a letter, talking about double letters, playing with spellings, and using analogies.

The following example illustrates how transcripts were coded. This interchange took place between Leah and the teacher, Ann, as they wrote about Filippo Brunelleschi, architect of Saint Mary of the Flower Church. Codes are enclosed within square brackets after each occurrence; a single example may have more than one code.[1]

LEAH: What if you said Filippo was a goldsmith # became, before he became # an architect, don't you think?

TEACHER: Okay, that's a good idea.

LEAH: Two L's? [talking about double letters, asking confirmation for part of word]

TEACHER: No, one L, two P's. [talking about double letters, contesting part of a word, spelling part of word]

LEAH: One L, I. [production]

TEACHER: Uh-huh, [confirming a letter] P-P-O, [production] and I never remember how to spell Brunelleschi. B-R-U-N-seleci, I think. [memory, negatively evaluating self as speller]

LEAH: B. [production]

TEACHER: R. [joint production]

LEAH: E? [joint production, asking confirmation of a letter]

TEACHER: Yeah, try it. [confirming a letter] It doesn't look right, does it? [checking by sight] Okay, let's not worry about it. [deferring concern about spelling] L-E-S-C-H-I, something like that. [production] We can figure it out another t // time. [deferring concern about spelling]

LEAH: That, I don't think so. [contesting part of a word]

TEACHER: I think there's an I. [spelling a letter] I think it's . . . no, it's . . . let's see. Something like that. I don't remember. [memory] Let's not waste time. [deferring concern about spelling] Okay, for many, many years Filippo Brunelleschi [typing] whoops.

Frequency of Spelling Talk. One unit of analysis employed in this study was what we call a *spelling episode*. An episode, like the example above, was defined as an exchange that centers on spelling. An episode begins when one person introduces spelling as a topic and continues until the topic is changed. A single episode, then, can include a number of utterances and speaking turns by both speakers. When children worked with each other, the number of episodes of spelling talk ranged from five to eighteen. The same children also collaborated twice with their teacher, during which the number of their spelling talk episodes ranged from four to eighteen. In the group as a whole, regardless of whether the partner was the teacher or another child, the range in the number of times that spelling was the topic of an exchange was similar, though the children's episodes were more extended, as evidenced by the fact that spelling was their third highest frequency category by utterance, whereas for the teacher it ranked seventh. Six children had more spelling episodes when they worked with their teacher, and ten talked about spelling more often with their peer partner.

We also measured the frequency of talk about spelling by counting the number of utterances (T-units) about spelling. A repeated-measures analysis of variance was conducted to examine whether there was a statistically significant difference in the amount of talk about spelling for the three groups studied (teacher talking to children, children talking to teacher, and children talking to each other). The analysis showed a significant group effect (F = 12.19, df = 2, 30; p < .0001). Follow-up analyses showed significant differences between all groups: children talking to teacher versus children talking to each other ($F[1,15]$ = 15.25, p < .001), teacher talking to children versus children talking to each other ($F[1,15]$ = 9.77, p < .001), and teacher talking to children versus children talking to teacher ($F[1,15]$ = 6.09, p < .03). That is, the teacher talked more about spelling than did her student partner when they worked together (teacher m = 11.0, student-to-teacher m = 8.2), but children talked more about spelling when they wrote with each other (student-to-student m = 25.7).

Teacher Talk About Spelling. The teacher used and modeled a wide range of spelling strategies when she worked with her students. In her talk, all but four of the thirty-four categories are represented: She did not ask her child partners to confirm her spelling of a word part or a particular letter, nor did she contest their spelling of either part of a word or the whole word. Of the thirty-four categories of spelling talk, the teacher had higher frequencies than did her students in twelve: spelling a word for the partner (either a whole word or part of one), confirming the spelling of a part of a word, negatively evaluating her own spelling, talking about morphemes, talking about rules or terms, telling the partner to defer concern for spelling until editing, checking spellings by sight and by meaning, talking about double letters, talking about an unusual word, and positively evaluating her partner's spelling.

Student Talk About Spelling. We found that all children used a broad range of categories. The only category not represented for a single child is positively evaluating the partner's spelling. Use of these different strategies displayed a wide frequency range, however, from a single time for using analogies and confirming spelling of a whole word to 193 instances of production.

For the children as a group, after the categories of production and joint production (106 instances of helping each other spell aloud), playing with spelling has the highest frequency (78 times). Like linguistic play in general (Daiute, 1989, 1990), this play can be seen as students' productive way of reflecting on and evaluating certain aspects of the spelling task. In their play around spelling, children analyzed sound-symbol relationships, compared different options for encoding both sound and meaning, and argued their points about which option to select. The following example illustrates how the children productively used play around spelling in their collaborations. In this episode, Andy and Russ have chosen to write about Christopher Columbus.

RUSS: Or Christopher Columbus the Spaniard, or the Spaniard Christopher Columbus, I don't know. Want me to wait?

ANDY: Span . . . you know how to spell that?

RUSS: I think . . .

ANDY: Wait . . . S-P-A-N-Y-R-E?

RUSS: Spaniard!

ANDY: I'm just gonna spell it, ha, like, you know so, it may not be right.

RUSS: Okay, because I already did none in, none in (?).

ANDY: The Spaniard, the Spaniard Christopher Columbus.

RUSS: Hey, I think you forgot to put in a [sound].

ANDY: Yeah, H.

RUSS: Christopher Columbus, Columbalumblus, Christopher, Christo-for.

ANDY: Yeah, I just . . .

RUSS: Christopher.

ANDY: [Simultaneously] Christopher.

RUSS: Oh, yeah.

ANDY: Christopher Columbus . . . see.

RUSS: I wonder when he found out the world was round.

RUSS: It should be last Friday or something [laugh].

ANDY: How do you spell, Colum. I don't know how to spell it. Help me start it out here.

RUSS: Uhh, U-L.

ANDY: Colum, yeah, you're right.

RUSS: M probably? I don't know. . . . Colllummbus, colllum, Christopher Cllm, Cllm.

ANDY: Christopher Columbus Collumm.

RUSS: Uh, I think B-U-S #. Yeah, something like that.

ANDY: B . . . I'm going to do B.

RUSS: It'll be on the bottom.

ANDY: Yeah, where # Columbus, Columbus # the Span // the Spaniard Christopher Columbus discovered America. Now do you know how to spell the last three letters of Christopher Columbus? Oh # I already asked you. Forget it.

RUSS: Actually, he rediscovered America.

ANDY: No, I-U-S.

RUSS: And he even made friends with some Indians.

Through such play, the boys have worked out the sound-symbol relationships and spelled Christopher Columbus correctly in their text. This example illustrates also that, while devoting a good deal of time and attention
to spelling, they confront high-level meaning issues, such as whether Columbus discovered or rediscovered America.

For the children as a whole, sounding out words also is an extremely
common strategy (73 instances), as are asking for the spelling of whole
words (47), talking about knowing or not knowing how to spell a word (43),
and asking the partner to confirm the spelling of part of a word (41).
Children's most frequent categories are producing, jointly producing, playing with spellings, sounding out, asking the spelling of a whole word, talking
about knowing (or not knowing) how to spell, and asking confirmation of the
spelling of part of a word.

It can be seen, then, that the teacher and students differed not only in frequency of talk about spelling but also in what they discussed. These differences between how the teacher and the students talked about spelling are
explored in the next section using a case study approach with three pairs of
students.

Case Studies of Young Writers and Spellers
During Peer Collaboration

We compared three pairs of children whom we classified as high, medium,
and low in spelling by using the grade equivalent (GE) score on the spelling
subtest of the California Achievement Test. This score represents the grade at
which the average child achieves a certain score. The first number is the
grade; the second is the month in that grade. In the sixth month of third grade,
the high pair both scored a grade equivalent of 6.5. The low spellers scored
2.9 and 3.4. The mixed ability pair scored 1.4 and 5.0. We define high and
low relative to the scores of this particular group of children, 60 percent of
whom scored above grade level on this test (median = 5.0). We acknowledge
that standardized tests present a very narrow picture of any child's ability.
Spelling scores are based on recognizing correctly spelled words; this proficiency may or may not reflect a student's own productive spelling. On the
other hand, spelling is a skill whose end point is production of a single correct
form, so this skill is perhaps better suited to standardized measures than are
more interpretive skills like drawing inferences. Furthermore, since this was
not planned as a study of spelling per se, we did not have alternative measures
to assess children's competence, such as scores on developmental spelling
inventories (Schlagal, 1989).

We describe here how the three pairs of children worked together and
the ways in which the teacher adjusted her interaction for spellers with different levels of ability.

High-High Pair. Leah and Mary had not only above-grade-level standardized test spelling scores (both 6.5) but also relatively low percentages of mis-spellings in their compositions: Leah ranged from 3 to 6 percent of total words, and Mary from 4 to 10 percent. In two collaborative sessions with each other, their misspelling rates were 7 percent and 9 percent. These percentages compare favorably with the 92 percent correct spelling rate for nine-year-olds found by Applebee, Langer, and Mullis (1987). For Leah and Mary, spelling is the third most frequent topic, after whom and what the story is about.

Both of these students had many more spelling episodes with their teacher than with each other. Together, the girls engaged in seven episodes of spelling talk. Leah had fourteen episodes with the teacher, and Mary had ten. Spelling more with the teacher was unusual; in the corpus as a whole, most children spelled more with each other. It may be that these two high-ability spellers had more to gain by talking with their teacher to acquire the more expert strategies that they needed.

Of the thirty-four categories of talk about spelling, Leah and Mary used nineteen. It is notable that sounding out is their highest frequency joint category, since spelling development research suggests that more able spellers do not rely on a sound-based strategy. Their incidence of production, that is spelling aloud, is very low.

Low-Low Pair. Shara and Emma had among the lowest standardized test spelling scores in the sample (GE 2.9 and 3.4, respectively). Percentages of misspellings in their compositions are greater than those of Leah and Mary. Shara ranged from 11 to 19 percent of total words, and Emma from 7 to 14 percent. In their two collaborative products, their misspelling rates were 14 percent and 18 percent.

For Shara and Emma, as for Leah and Mary, spelling is the third most frequent topic, after whom and what the story is about. Emma had more spelling episodes with Shara, whereas Shara had more with the teacher. The girls had eleven joint episodes of spelling talk. Emma had nine with the teacher, and Shara had thirteen.

Of the thirty-four categories of talk about spelling, Shara and Emma used thirteen. Contradicting what would be expected from the spelling literature, they relied less on the sounding out strategy than did Leah and Mary, but other sound-based categories were represented, such as spelling by syllables and types of play that involved the sounds of words.

High-Low Pair. Brant's standardized test spelling score (GE 1.4) placed him two years below grade level. Gary's score (GE 5.0) was almost as much above grade level. Percentages of misspellings in their individual compositions reflect a similar disparity. Brant ranged from 8 to 31 percent, whereas Gary ranged from 2 to 7 percent. In two collaborative sessions, their misspelling rates were 8 percent and 3 percent, showing the influence of Gary's input.

Gary and Brant talked more about spelling than about any other topic, though Brant's frequency of spelling talk was greater than that of his partner.

Both boys had more spelling episodes with each other than with their teacher, showing the influence of Brant's keen interest in talking about spelling. Brant's insistence on talking about spelling was also shown by the fact that, as measured by utterance, he talked more about spelling than did the teacher, although, overall, she talked much more than he did.

Of the thirty-four categories of talk about spelling, Gary and Brant used twenty-two. The extent to which each relied on sounding out differed, with Brant using it heavily (seventeen times, the highest frequency in the entire sample) and Gary hardly at all (three times). Also, Brant made frequent use of the play strategy.

Case Studies of Young Writers and Spellers Working with the Teacher

In addition to analyzing how these pairs of children worked together, we also assessed how the teacher interacted with children of different spelling abilities as they talked about spelling as one aspect of the writing task.

High-Ability Spellers. When the teacher worked with the better spellers, the interaction was different from most teacher-student interactions in classrooms. It was much closer to conversation than to teacher-student talk in several ways. For instance, the category of joint production, where partners spell together, was highest for the teacher when working with Leah and Mary, showing collaborative spelling. Asking questions was evenly distributed among speakers; the teacher asked authentic questions, as when she questioned the spelling of the name of the princess in the class play. The following exchange exemplifies the character of the conversation:

MARY: How do you spell completion?
TEACHER: E . . . no one E . . . T-I-O-N.

Although Mary asked how to spell a whole word, the teacher supplied only the hard part, much as one would for another adult. Similarly, when Leah was spelling *finally*, the teacher merely said, "Two L's," and Leah replied, "That's what I thought."

In addition, the usual role of teacher as supplier of information was reversed because the teacher asked Leah and Mary how to spell entire words; she did not make such requests of the less able spellers. Furthermore, the teacher modeled spelling awareness for the good spellers by commenting on her own errors or words that give her trouble. For instance, when Leah was trying to spell *success,* the teacher remarked, "It's one of those words that, you know what? To this day I'm never sure." Such comments may help students to develop a "spelling conscience," that is, to know when a word may be wrong, a skill that is considered very important for proficient spelling (Block and Peskowitz, 1990). Such awareness can be related to proofreading and also to the use of resources to help with difficult spellings. In addition, with these more able spellers, the teacher modeled the use of meaning to check spellings more than she did with the other children.

When working with the more able spellers, the teacher was more apt to provide spellings, both whole words and parts of them. It may be that she felt that they did not need the practice of working out spellings as required by lower-ability spellers. Furthermore, she provided high-level information, as when she used an etymological explanation in the following:

TEACHER: How 'bout something like "performance was in the auditorium"?
LEAH: A-T?
TEACHER: A-U-D.
LEAH: A.
TEACHER: U-D. Aud // kind of like audio means things that you hear.

Low-Ability Spellers. When working with the children who had the most trouble with spelling, the teacher assumed a more "traditional teacher" voice and provided more direct instruction. She monitored their spelling more, saying things like "Check out how you spelled *with;* you have one extra H in there" and "That says hospitile, T-A-L is hospital, T-A-L."

A very high frequency category of teacher talk when working with the less able spellers related to checking spellings by sight. Checking by reading was also modeled, for instance, when a spelling produced a wrong word, as in "Many *moths* have passed" instead of "Many *months* have passed." Visual factors have been shown to become increasingly important as spellers develop (Tenney, 1980); incorporation of visual information is considered an indication of progress according to stage theories of spelling development. Therefore, the teacher may have been trying to promote a skill that she felt these less able spellers needed in order to go beyond their own sound-based systems. So, when the teacher said to Emma, "Sometimes words just don't look right," she was modeling an important strategy. The teacher also made more frequent reference to spelling rules with Shara and Emma.

When the teacher worked with Brant, the lowest ability speller, she spelled throughout. She joined him in using a sounding out strategy. When Brant was trying to write *frustrating,* she helped him with the following: "It's a frrrrruss, fru fru." She also told him how to spell words before he asked, perhaps as a way to minimize his attention to them. Brant's concern about spelling was evident in the frequency with which he talked about spelling and in his remark, spoken when he was told to defer worry about spelling until editing, "We want to be correct the first time." Some researchers have raised doubts about the practice of not answering young children's questions about spelling, a practice that is common among teachers who promote invented spelling (Bruneau, Rasinski, and Ambrose, 1990; Schickedanz, 1990). In our study, the teacher's increased support of Brant's spelling during composing, rather than at the editing stage where she concentrated help for the others, may reflect a similar concern about his potential frustration. While editing, she directed his attention to serious errors like the wrong homonym of *wood/would* and *trash* spelled with no vowel.

Conclusion

When given the choice about what to talk about as they composed, children allocated a good deal of their discussion to spelling. Their talk revealed a wide assortment of strategies that they used to encode words, though they also devoted attention to the meaning and organization of what they wanted to write. Other analyses based on these data show that the children used each other and the teacher as resources for a variety of types of support. One kind of support that they consistently sought (and provided for each other) was help with the process of spelling.

In this study, we found that the amount of talk about spelling did not vary according to the spelling ability of the children. In an interview study of children's use of strategies, Radebaugh (1985) found that good spellers mentioned a larger number of strategies. However, like Wilde (1988), we found that the numbers of strategies used by spellers of different abilities were similar, regardless of spelling ability level as measured by a standardized test and by the percentage of errors in their writing. Furthermore, while there were some differences in which categories of spelling talk children used, across ability groups there were not striking contrasts.

On the other hand, the interactions between the teacher and students of different spelling abilities were more distinct. The teacher appeared to tailor her support to her partner's level in ways that were quite subtle, though obvious upon analysis. One way to view these discussions about spelling is to see them as scaffolding, with the teacher aiming her instruction at both the child's current level of achievement and also at the next logical step for increased spelling proficiency. While this finding does not preclude the necessity for what Clay and Cazden (1990, p. 216) call "instructional detours," in which spelling is sometimes taught in isolation, it does argue for the conclusion that spelling instruction can take place in the context of writing activities. Another discovery that relates to spelling instruction is that use of memory is one of the least frequent categories, with only five instances in the entire sample. This finding is interesting because memorization has historically been and continues to be the most common way of teaching spelling (Barone, 1992; Morris, 1989; Seda, 1989). This study suggests that in actual composition, neither the children nor the teacher chose to rely on memory (or at least to talk about doing so). Perhaps providing strategies instead of answers, as the teacher did, is more productive.

Recommendations for Further Research

The children in this study frequently talked about spelling, yet they also discussed many other aspects of the writing process and thus appeared able to integrate their concern about encoding with attention to meaning and form. As evidence of this integration, we offer the frequency and range of other topics that the children and their teacher talked about. We consider this largely descriptive study to be a beginning attempt to study spelling in context. For future research on spelling strategies, we recommend an outcomes measure for written products to further substantiate our finding that children's attention to spelling need not detract from their attention to other important aspects of composing. We do not have independent quality ratings of students' compositions because of the variety of topics offered to the children and the diversity of genres that they produced.

In keeping with the goal of this study, we recommend research that explores new ways of conceptualizing literacy behaviors that are more complex than the layered notion of higher and lower skills (or stages). Reading and writing involve the orchestration of multiple tasks, of which spelling is an important one, especially for children. Therefore, we need research that helps us to understand how writers and readers make sense of the simultaneous demands of and influences on many aspects of literacy. Spelling must be considered in the light of sociocultural issues like the language background of the child, sociopolitical issues like the ways in which literacy has been used in a community to privilege or discriminate, sociocognitive issues like knowledge of word families, and neurolinguistic issues like whether a student is among the small number of children whose literacy practices are influenced by neurological problems. Research about how writers make sense of and through written language must address encoding in relation to these other issues.

Note

1. The following transcript codes are used in this chapter: # = pause, // = self-correction, (?) = unclear word or words, . . . = trailing off.

References

Applebee, A. W., Langer, J. A., and Mullis, I. V. *Grammar, Punctuation, and Spelling: Controlling Conventions of Written English at Ages Nine, Thirteen, and Seventeen.* Princeton, N.J.: Educational Testing Service, 1987. (ED 282 928)

Barone, D. "Whatever Happened to Spelling?: The Role of Instruction in Process-Centered Classrooms." *Reading Psychology*, 1992, *13*, 1–17.

Beers, J. W. "Developmental Strategies of Spelling Competence in Primary School Children." In E. H. Henderson and J. W. Beers (eds.), *Developmental and Cognitive Aspects of Learning to Spell: A Reflection of Word Knowledge.* Newark, Del.: International Reading Association, 1980.

Beers, J. W., and Henderson, E. H. "A Study of Developing Orthographic Concepts Among First Graders." *Research in the Teaching of English*, 1977, *11*, 133–148.

94   THE DEVELOPMENT OF LITERACY THROUGH SOCIAL INTERACTION

Blazer, B. " 'I Want to Talk to You About Writing': Five-Year-Old Children Speak." In B. B. Schiefflin and P. Gilmore (eds.), *The Acquisition of Literacy: Ethnographic Perspectives.* Norwood, N.J.: Ablex, 1986.

Block, K. K., and Peskowitz, N. B. "Metacognition and Spelling: Using Writing and Reading to Self-Check Spelling." *Elementary School Journal,* 1990, *91,* 151–164.

Bouffler, C. "Spelling: The Myths and the Reality." In D. Burnes, H. French, and F. Moore (eds.), *Literacy: Strategies and Perspectives.* Sydney: Australian Reading Association, 1985.

Bouffler, C. "Spelling Development." *Australian Journal of Reading,* 1991, *14,* 307–316.

Bruneau, B. J., Rasinski, T. V., and Ambrose, R. P. "Parents' Perceptions of Children's Reading and Writing Development in a Whole Language Kindergarten Program." In J. Zutell and S. McCormick (eds.), *Literacy Theory and Research: Analyses from Multiple Paradigms.* Thirty-Ninth Yearbook of the National Reading Conference. Chicago: National Reading Conference, 1990.

Buchanan, E. *Spelling for Whole Language Classrooms.* Winnipeg, Canada: Whole Language Consultants, 1989.

Chall, J. S. *Stages of Reading Development.* New York: McGraw-Hill, 1983.

Chomsky, C. "Invented Spelling in the Open Classroom." *Word,* 1971, *127,* 499–518.

Clay, M. M., and Cazden, C. B. "A Vygotskian Interpretation of Reading Recovery." In L. C. Moll (ed.), *Vygotsky and Education: Instructional Implications and Applications of Sociohistorical Psychology.* New York: Cambridge University Press, 1990.

Cordeiro, P. "Children's Punctuation: An Analysis of Errors in Period Placement." *Research in the Teaching of English,* 1988, *22,* 62–75.

Daiute, C. "Play as Thought: Thinking Strategies of Young Writers." *Harvard Educational Review,* 1989, *59,* 1–23.

Daiute, C. "The Role of Play in Writing Development." *Research in the Teaching of English,* 1990, *24,* 4–47.

Daiute, C., and Dalton, B. " 'Let's Brighten It Up a Bit': Collaboration and Cognition in Writing." In B. Rafoth and D. Rubin (eds.), *The Social Construction of Writing.* Norwood, N.J.: Ablex, 1988.

Downing, J., DiStephano, J., Rich, G., and Bell, A. "Children's Views of Spelling." *Elementary School Journal,* 1984, *85,* 185–198.

Dyson, A. H. *Multiple Worlds of Child Writers: Friends Learning to Write.* New York: Teachers College Press, 1989.

Ehri, L. C. "Review and Commentary: Stages of Spelling Development." In S. Templeton and D. R. Bear (eds.), *Development of Orthographic Knowledge and the Foundations of Literacy: A Memorial Festschrift to Edmund H. Henderson.* Hillsdale, N.J.: Erlbaum, 1992.

Gentry, J. R. "Early Spelling Strategies." *Elementary School Journal,* 1978, *79,* 88–92.

Gentry, J. R. "An Analysis of Invented Spelling in *Gnys at Wrk.*" *The Reading Teacher,* 1982, *35,* 192–200.

Gentry, J. R., and Gillet, J. W. *Teaching Kids to Spell.* Portsmouth, N.H.: Heinemann Educational Books, 1993.

Goodman, K. *What's Whole in Whole Language?* Portsmouth, N.H.: Heinemann Educational Books, 1986.

Graves, D. H. *Writing: Teachers and Children at Work.* Portsmouth, N.H.: Heinemann Educational Books, 1983.

Henderson, E. H. "Developmental Concepts of Word." In E. H. Henderson and J. W. Beers (eds.), *Developmental and Cognitive Aspects of Learning to Spell: A Reflection of Word Knowledge.* Newark, Del.: International Reading Association.

Henderson, E. H., and Beers, J. W. (eds.). *Developmental and Cognitive Aspects of Learning to Spell: A Reflection of Word Knowledge.* Newark, Del.: International Reading Association, 1980.

Henderson, E. H., and Templeton, S. "A Developmental Perspective of Formal Spelling Instruction Through Alphabet, Patterns, and Meaning." *Elementary School Journal,* 1986, *86,* 304–316.

LaBerge, D., and Samuels, S. J. "Toward a Theory of Automatic Information Processing in Reading." *Cognitive Psychology*, 1974, *6*, 293–323.

McGee, L. M., and Richgels, D. J. *Literacy's Beginnings: Supporting Young Readers and Writers*. Needham Heights, Mass.: Allyn & Bacon, 1990.

Marsh, G., Friedman, M., Welch, V., and Desberg, P. "The Development of Strategies in Spelling." In U. Frith (ed.), *Cognitive Processes in Spelling*. San Diego: Academic Press, 1980.

Morris, D. "Editorial Comment: Developmental Spelling Theory Revisited." *Reading Psychology*, 1989, *10*, iii–ix.

Radebaugh, M. R. "Children's Perceptions of Their Spelling Strategies." *The Reading Teacher*, 1985, *38*, 532–536.

Read, C. "Children's Perceptions of the Sounds of English: Phonology from Three to Six." Unpublished doctoral dissertation, Graduate School of Education, Harvard University, 1970.

Read, C. "Preschool Children's Knowledge of English Phonology." *Harvard Educational Review*, 1971, *41*, 1–34.

Read, C. *Children's Creative Spelling*. London: Routledge & Kegan Paul, 1986.

Schickedanz, J. A. *Adam's Righting Revolutions: One Child's Literacy Development from Infancy Through Grade One*. Portsmouth, N.H.: Heinemann Educational Books, 1990.

Schlagal, R. C. "Constancy and Change in Spelling Development." *Reading Psychology*, 1989, *10*, 207–232.

Schlagal, R. C. "Patterns of Orthographic Development into the Intermediate Grades." In S. Templeton and D. R. Bear (eds.), *Development of Orthographic Knowledge and the Foundations of Literacy: A Memorial Festschrift to Edmund H. Henderson*. Hillsdale, N.J.: Erlbaum, 1992.

Scibior, O. "Reconsidering Spelling Development: A Socio-Psycholinguistic Perspective." Unpublished doctoral dissertation, School of Education, Indiana University, 1987.

Seda, M. "Examining the Proverbial Gap Between Spelling Research and the Practice of Spelling in American Classrooms." *Reading Improvement*, 1989, *26*, 315–322.

Shaughnessy, M. P. *Errors and Expectations: A Guide for the Teacher of Basic Writing*. New York: Oxford University Press, 1977.

Templeton, S. "Young Children Invent Words: Developing Concepts of 'Wordness.' " *The Reading Teacher*, 1980, *33*, 454–459.

Templeton, S. "Theory, Nature, and Pedagogy of Higher-Order Orthographic Development in Older Students." In S. Templeton and D. R. Bear (eds.), *Development of Orthographic Knowledge and the Foundations of Literacy: A Memorial Festschrift to Edmund H. Henderson*. Hillsdale, N.J.: Erlbaum, 1992.

Tenney, Y. J. "Visual Factors in Spelling." In U. Frith (ed.), *Cognitive Processes in Spelling*. San Diego: Academic Press, 1980.

Venezky, R. L. "Notes on the History of English Spelling." *Visible Language*, 1976, *10*, 351–365.

Vygotsky, L. S. *Mind in Society: The Development of Higher Psychological Processes*. (M. Cole, V. John-Steiner, S. Scribner, and E. Souberman, eds.) Cambridge, Mass.: Harvard University Press, 1978.

Wilde, S. "Learning to Spell and Punctuate: A Study of Eight- and Nine-Year-Old Children." *Language and Education*, 1988, *2*, 35–59.

Wilde, S. "Looking at Invented Spelling: A Kidwatcher's Guide, Part 1"; "Understanding Spelling Strategies: A Kidwatcher's Guide, Part 2." In K. S. Goodman, Y. M. Goodman, and W. J. Hood (eds.), *The Whole Language Evaluation Book*. Portsmouth, N.H.: Heinemann Educational Books, 1989.

Wilde, S. *YOU KAN RED THIS!: Spelling and Punctuation for Whole Language Classrooms, K–6*. Portsmouth, N.H.: Heinemann Educational Books, 1992.

Zutell, J. "Spelling Strategies of Primary School Children and Their Relationship to Piaget's Concept of Decentration." *Research in the Teaching of English*, 1979, *13*, 69–80.

MAUREEN REDDY is a doctoral candidate in language and literacy at the Graduate School of Education, Harvard University.

COLETTE DAIUTE is associate professor at the Graduate School of Education, Harvard University.

Written narrative activities can serve children as they make sense of academic material and academic life, thereby expanding writing as a mode of learning that includes affective and social as well as cognitive capacities in the child.

The Social Construction of Written Narratives

Colette Daiute, Terri M. Griffin

This chapter focuses on children's written narratives, in particular children's use of written narratives to make sense of academic material and events in their school lives. Our work on children's written narratives extends research on the development of oral narratives. Such research has shown how children use linguistic devices to reflect their interpretations and feelings about poignant events in their lives. Written narratives, like oral narratives, may also serve such sense-making functions, but this function of children's writing has not yet been explored as an important dimension of literacy.

When children write narratives incorporating school subject matter, they can use narrative as a mode of learning. In their written narratives, children can construct and reflect on academic material in the same way that they interpret their personal experiences. When writing stories about historical events, for example, children can interpret these events, as did Andy and Russ, two third-grade boys who wrote the following news story.

The spanyard Christopher Columbus rediscovered the west Indies thinking it was Japan. This was a great challenge for Mr. Columbus and his crew. Mr. Columbus was very proud that he and his crew had found the new world.

He met new natives in the new world. He learn new things from the natives as well as the natives learned new things from them.

When writing this story for the class newspaper, Andy and Russ pretended to go back in time and report on a discovery during the Renaissance. In doing so, they interpreted historical events by conveying characters' thoughts and feelings (*thinking it was Japan, a great challenge, very proud*) and by making the point that Columbus rediscovered the West Indies—a point that the boys discussed at length together when they wrote the story and that they explored further by portraying the natives' perspective as well as that of Columbus. Through the act of story writing, these children, like others, empathized with historical characters in a way that integrated history, which often involves rote memorization of facts, into their own experience. Although Andy and Russ's narrative might not be rated very high on mechanics or clarity, it engaged the children with academic material in affective, cognitive, and cultural ways, as they presented information, organized it in narrative form, and empathized with characters' perspectives. Such empathy, as we demonstrate in this chapter, is a much more important aspect of children's writing in school than has previously been recognized.

The view of children's writing presented here differs from the more typical approach of examining children's literacy as a set of skills. According to our theory, children's writing, like their storytelling about events in their lives, should be examined as a way of understanding their perspectives on academic matters, rather than only as an indication of their cultural and linguistic skills. Thus, narrative writing in school is important for its interpretive function.

Our research is grounded in the premise that children develop their own personal discourse modes based on day-to-day interactions in a variety of contexts, including interactions with peers and teachers as well as with parents and others in their home cultures. Our research is consistent with the understanding that narrative forms are constructed in relation to the mores and discourse patterns of ethnic, racial, class, and other types of cultures. In our work, we attempt to extend notions of cultural construction to explore how children and teachers interact with each other and with texts in their classrooms. Classrooms that are rich in social interaction, like the one where Andy and Russ wrote their story, engage children in the use of discourse styles that move beyond their home discourse and beyond traditional school discourse. A major element of classrooms where children can truly make sense of the curriculum is peer interaction, which links culture and development, since it involves children in interpreting academic material in their own ways.

With respect to developmental and cultural aspects of written narrative, we are exploring two ideas about the nature of written narratives and the social construction of narratives in classroom settings: (1) Children use written narrative to construct and interpret academic material and other aspects of school life. (2) Children construct academic narrative discourse form in complex ways in the classroom that parallel the social construction of discourse in other cultural contexts. When creating written narratives with a teacher, children have access to the privileged discourse model of the school culture, and when children write narratives with peers, they have the opportunity to impose their own strategies and interpretations on school tasks. In our study, we explored the social and personal construction of narratives by contrasting narrative texts and composing sessions by teacher-child and peer pairs as they related to the work of individual children across time.

Development of Oral Narratives

Research on oral narratives about salient personal events, like one's involvement in an accident, has shown that children's stories reflect their self-concepts and their attempts to make sense of the social and physical worlds in which they live (Bruner, 1986; Labov and Waletsky, 1967; McCabe and Peterson, 1991). Researchers have shown how children across age groups shape narratives and employ specific linguistic devices to convey their evaluations of events and characters in their stories. Rather than being objective descriptions of events, children's narratives offer the subjective stances of the child narrators in the form of discourse features such as verbs of emotion ("I *felt scared* as the bee was flying around my head"), internal states ("I *heard* the bee flying around my head"), qualifiers that mark intensity with adjectives and adverbs ("The bee was *very* close to me"), repetitions ("The bee was *buzz, buzz, buzzing* around my head"), exclamations (*Buzz!!!*), and other features. By using these and other devices, the child is not only recounting but also interpreting an event, telling what the event meant to him or her.

Research on oral narratives has shown that storytelling strategies emerge in cultural contexts, within groups of storytellers and listeners (McCabe, 1992). Diverse groups shape narratives and reveal their interpretations in different ways. People in Western, white cultures tend to tell event-driven narratives that set the scene, revolve around a conflict or problem, and come to some kind of resolution at the end. In contrast, African American storytellers often present series of anecdotes with overlapping themes, and Latino narrators may assume a more character-based approach by casting stories in the contexts of relationships (Heath, 1983; McCabe, 1992; Rodino and others, 1991). The nature and extent of storytelling within the family also have an impact on whether and how children adopt the storytelling model in their culture, with some parents engaging their children in remembering and talking about past events, and other parents modeling different forms of interaction (Hudson, Gebelt, Haviland, and Bentivegna, 1992). Influenced by these and other cultural patterns, storytellers also have ways of projecting their own points of view on the events, characters, and themes in their stories.

According to Bakhtin (1986), each person's discourse is influenced by the speech styles of the many communities in which he or she has participated, including his or her culture, family, and academic discipline. This notion of "speech genre"—the specialized discourse form of a group—can also be extended to include children's styles of interacting with teachers and peers (Daiute, 1993), as well as with parents and other representatives of the broader culture. Yet there has been little exploration into how narratives and other genres are constructed during classroom discourse (Snow and Dickinson, 1990). While teachers' controlling and rigid classroom discourse styles have been studied (Cazden, 1988; Mehan, 1979; Michaels, 1991), researchers have only begun to examine how socially mediated classrooms with extensive conversation between teachers and children might allow for diverse influences on the development of narrative and other discourse forms.

Theoretical Context for Research on Written Narratives Around School Subjects

Children's reactions to academic material and school activities have not been considered in literacy research, yet learning school "stuff" requires that children make sense of it in their own terms. A large part of what children may be doing when they construct new knowledge is reacting to facts and concepts as they fit them into stories. This idea that narratives might provide interpretative and mnemonic frameworks for academic material is consistent with schema theory and research, which explains that children read and remember material better when they already know something about the topic (Bransford, Vye, Adams, and Perfetto, 1989). Although schema theory has been explored in relation to conceptual knowledge frameworks (Schank and Abelson, 1977), the notion that personally meaningful stories might provide a useful context for school learning has not been explored in any detail. The reason why narrative might be a useful academic context, moreover, is that it involves interpretation as well as structural support. Thus, rather than write a report about living conditions in the Renaissance, Andy and Russ, in the earlier cited example, took a stance on the facts as they wrote their news story. Determining relationships between such a process and children's fact recall would eventually be required to extend our argument, but, at this point, an understanding of the nature of the narrative context for children's affective, cognitive, and cultural meaning making can offer evidence to shift theoretical paradigms away from the overly cognitive focus that has dominated educational research.

Written narratives, like spoken narratives, can capture children's perceptions and feelings about the world around them (Fox, 1991). Exploration of the sense making and affective aspects of children's writing about school subjects can offer invaluable information about children's strategies for interpreting and mastering school material as well as information about any affective resources or barriers that they bring to this material. We extended the narrative domain by asking children to write stories including events and characters that they had studied in history and science and that pertained to contemporary issues in their communities and in their own lives. In this way, children write narratives for the purpose of learning as well as for communication.

In order to consider the sense-making functions of writing stories in school, researchers and educators need to shift from evaluating the structure and correctness of children's narratives to examining how children evaluate subject matter, events, characters, and themselves in the stories they write and in the conversations they have around literacy activities. This focus on meaning and affect within narrative theory differs from most examinations of written language, which tend to focus on the structures and processes of reading and writing. Children have more difficulty creating written than oral language so the sophistication of evaluation devices in writing may lag behind those in oral narratives. Nevertheless, our examination shows how children's writing, even about school subjects, reflects their points of view.

Our research examines the classroom as a context where children create narratives. Children's narratives are clearly influenced by the discourse patterns in their home cultures, but the classroom is also a culture in which the teacher and peer group convey discourse patterns and values. Researchers have noted hidden mismatches between teachers' and students' discourse patterns (Delpit, 1988; Michaels, 1991), and researchers have argued for explicit treatment of discourse patterns as a way of more clearly providing all children with access to classroom discourse (Cazden, 1992; Delpit, 1988). Yet, we know very little about the nature or impact of various types of instruction around discourse forms like narrative, regardless of how explicit the instruction may be. We need to find out how discourse forms are constructed by teachers and children in classrooms in order to appreciate the role of the classroom as a context for social construction of narrative and children's experience as learners. Theoretically compelling proposals have been offered by sociocultural theorists, including Bakhtin (1986), whose notion of speech genres has provided a tool for seeing the diverse patterns of thought and expression. This notion that each person's discourse is composed of utterances from the cultures in which he or she has interacted implies a broad notion of culture. These broad strokes do not, however, offer information about how individual children make sense of and transform public speech genres for their own use.

The goal of our research is to consider affective and social factors in children's writing because these may provide insights about how to increase children's access to literacy and learning. We take a descriptive approach to explore the hypothesis that children's narrative texts and narrative construction processes often differ from those of their teachers. We hypothesize that these differences revolve around issues of narrative structure and sense making. Several questions about the nature of children's written narratives and composing processes around narrative writing activities in the elementary classroom form the basis of our inquiry: What are the structural and affective features of written narratives composed by children working in a variety of situations: with a teacher, with a peer, and individually? What is the nature of the narrative construction process when children work with a teacher and with a peer? What do the processes and products of written narrative construction among children and their teacher in a third-grade classroom indicate about how children construe school-based literacy tasks?

Methods and Analyses

Contrasting teacher-student and peer interaction around the construction of written narratives provides insights into different social spheres of classroom discourse. Previous research has indicated that children use developmentally appropriate strategies to improve their writing when they work with peers, though such strategies as play and associative language differ markedly from the strategies of experienced writers and teachers (Daiute, 1990; Daiute and Dalton, 1993; Daiute, Campbell, Griffin, Reddy, and Tivnan, this volume). The present study involves similar contrasts and relates these different instructional speech genres to the development of written narratives by different groups of collaborators.

The methods of this study were the same as those described in Daiute, Campbell, Griffin, Reddy, and Tivnan (this volume) and Reddy and Daiute (this volume). The analyses for this study, however, focused on narrative writing skills. We focused on stories that sixteen children and their teacher wrote for a class newspaper reporting on events that the children had studied about the Renaissance and on events in their classroom. The children were asked to play the role of Renaissance chroniclers and modern-day news reporters to report on events that they deemed worthy, including the completion of Brunelleschi's dome on the cathedral in Florence, Italy, a meeting of merchants who were trying to deal with the city trash problem, a noble family's move to a new palace, and an invention or discovery in the Renaissance. The children also chose five contemporary events in their classroom life as topics for news stories, including the accident in which a classmate broke his leg, the class trip to the Gardner Museum, a class art exhibit, and children's participation in musical activities. The story prompts asked children to tell what happened and to write why the event was important, as well as to include, if possible, two related vocabulary words (see Daiute, Campbell, Griffin, Reddy, and Tivnan, this volume, for the story prompts and research design). Each child wrote five stories individually, some before and some after collaborating twice with the teacher and twice with the same peer.

Text Analyses. This study yielded 128 written narratives: 80 texts written individually by children before and after composing collaboratively with the teacher and a peer, 32 texts written by teacher-child pairs, and 16 texts written by peer pairs. The narrative analysis included (1) high-point and evaluation analyses to determine the structure of and interpretive devices in the 128 texts (Labov and Waletzky, 1967; Labov, 1972; Miranda, Camp, Hemphill, and Wolf, 1992; Peterson and McCabe, 1983) and (2) a focalization analysis created for this study.

The high-point analysis involved describing the narrative function of each major clause, including orientation, complicating actions, evaluations, resolutions, abstracts, and codas (Peterson and McCabe, 1983). In addition to noting clause-by-clause narrative functions, we also described the overall structure of each narrative. Depending on the nature and arrangement of narrative clause functions, a narrative might be coded as classic, chronology, chronology with evaluation, event sequences (typically one-event, two-event, or three-event sequences), or miscellaneous. Peterson and McCabe (1983) developed this narrative coding scheme in the context of Standard English, and since the children in our study were from a variety of cultural groups (five African Americans, one Asian American, one Indian American, and nine European Americans) and economic groups (range from low to high income), we were sensitive to alternative narrative structures (McCabe, 1992). We modified the Peterson and McCabe (1983) scoring scheme to address issues that emerged in our written narrative data, which included the teacher's standard written English discourse forms and some diverse discourse patterns across children, as we describe below in the discussion of our results. For example, the written narrative task allowed for more complexity in narrative tense, including the present tense for reporting on events, character thoughts, and so on. In addition, the authors in our study often achieved resolutions via evaluation statements that provided closure for a story, as in the following excerpt from a narrative written by Dorina and her teacher about a Renaissance celebration:

> Jugglers were there and the jesters kept everybody laughing. Minstrels who were playing harps and lutes told exciting stories and sang beautiful songs. All the people who attended agreed that this was a great celebration.

Thus, our coding was more liberal in assigning the functions of complicating action, resolution, and evaluation than was the original high-point analysis.

It is important to note here that our emphasis on the teacher's classic form as a reference point does not imply that the classic form is right or that the children's narrative styles are not important. Rather, since we were exploring how cultural construction of narratives occurs and the teacher defines the privileged culture in the classroom, we used her model as a reference point. A more important point for us, however, was that cultural transmission is mediated greatly by children's narrative styles, whether they reflect family backgrounds, developmental status, or personal styles. Children's evaluations in their narratives and their focus on meaning as they wrote reveal their styles, incorporating the myriad cultural influences on their oral language.

Since examining affect was of central interest in this study, the evaluation analysis was expanded to assess children's use of evaluation within clauses (Miranda, Camp, Hemphill, and Wolf, 1992) and their use of special devices of written language, such as exclamation points, capital letters, and enlarged print size as markers of intensification, was added for this study. Evaluations included subjective states (internal states of emotion such as "She was mad" and cognition such as "I think that was . . . "); physical states ("She was tired"); intentions ("She tried to go"); qualifiers (intensifiers, delimiters, negation, adjectives, and adverbs); linguistic devices reflecting the author's evaluation, such as repetition ("She was so so mad") and exaggeration ("I hit the ball out of the park"); and causality ("He went there because he had no money, or because he was lonesome").

The focalization analysis indicated how authors expressed and controlled point of view in the narratives (Bal, 1991; Bamberg, 1991). Since high-point analysis was developed to code oral narratives of personal experiences, the point of view was assumed to be the speaker's. Analysis of children's writing requires accounting for a variety of points of view, including those of characters, the author, and the narrator. The focalization analysis involved determining whether children portrayed information in their narratives with relatively more or less distance, as indicated by the level of specificity and the use of evaluation. For example, this analysis distinguished among relatively external and internal stances assumed by the author, such as the external stance of an omniscient author in "Once upon a time, there was a city in Italy" compared to the internal stance taken by the author when privy to a character's feelings or internal states, as in "Brunelleschi was happy to be working on the dome."

The focalization analysis also captured the extent to which the author was explicitly present in the story, as in "I was walking along a street in Renaissance Italy when . . . ," compared to telling a story about events in the Renaissance. The child's attributions of internal, subjective states to third-person characters and in their own first-person reporting were distinguished, since such third-person reporting might reflect increasing control over a variety of types of narrative expression. By having characters such as the Renaissance architect Brunelleschi evaluate events in their lives, the children demonstrated control over subject matter and the text as well as used the text and writing for their own self-expression. The categories of focalization included external focus, including distant focus and author-observer, and internal focus, including author-character focus, character focus, and unspecified focus (distinguished by the position of evaluation in the text). The major distinction between external and internal focus is evaluation in the text, and subdivisions of each mark distance or attribution of evaluation.

Analyses of Narrative Composing Sessions. The study yielded forty-eight transcripts of composing sessions by teacher-student pairs (thirty-two forty-five-minute sessions) and peer pairs (sixteen forty-five-minute sessions). The narrative script analysis captured the paradigmatic (Hymes, 1972) structures of the discussion around narrative features during collaborative composing. Script analyses for teacher-student and peer composing sessions were developed by noting the recurrent patterns that speakers used to discuss narrative features as they composed. The specific teacher-child and peer scripts that emerged from our analysis are reported as results.

Results and Interpretation

Our analyses of the narrative texts and conversations as the teacher and children created those texts revealed a major contrast between the teacher's and children's approaches to narrative writing. The teacher guided children toward creating narrative texts of the classic type (Peterson and McCabe, 1983) and organized composing sessions with children around structural features of narrative. In contrast, the children tended to use written narratives to interpret the task, to explore issues in the language arts curriculum that were of concern to them, and to experiment with new academic content related to the task. In brief, the analyses revealed differences in emphases: structure by the teacher, and sense—personal meaning—by the children.

Narrative Structure. As shown in Table 6.1, results of the high-point analysis indicated that the teacher engaged her students in constructing mostly classic narratives, with 56 percent of the teacher-student texts in classic form and 25 percent in the form of chronology with evaluation, which has all the features of a classic narrative except a clear resolution. Few of the teacher-student texts were mere chronologies (9 percent) or three-event narratives (9 percent), and none were two-event narratives or narratives that ended at the high point.

The following is an example of a narrative in the classic form, written by the teacher and an Asian American male student, Andy. The authors wrote about the trash problem during the Renaissance and how a group of merchants tried to deal with this problem. In their story, Andy and his teacher described the gravity of the problem and discussed how this problem affected people's lives, and the fact that the merchants were unable to come up with a solution. This story involves orienting clauses, complicating actions, and a

Table 6.1. Percentage Distribution of
Written Narratives, by Type

Narrative Structure Types	Teacher-Child (N = 32)	Peer (N = 16)	Individual (N = 80)
Classic	.56	.13	.08
End at high point	0	0	.03
Chronology with evaluation	.25	.19	.15
Chronology	.09	.13	.14
Three-event narrative	.09	.31	.16
Two-event narrative	0	0	.19
One-event narrative	0	.13	.14
Miscellaneous	0	.13	.13

Note: Columns do not add up to 100 percent due to rounding.

resolution, albeit a temporary one that does not solve the overall problem even though it resolves the action in the specific events of the text.

> The merchants are finally trying to put an end to the horrible problem of trash. The terrible aroma makes people ill. People are buying perfume by the gallons in an attempt to hide the smell. The trash is piled so high on all the streets and it looks disgraceful. Horrble rats are climbing all over the trash and having a feast. The filthy rats make the town look even more disgraceful.
>
> The angry merchants feel that the garbage is affecting their business. After all, no one would want to come to a dirty, smelly, rat infested town. The merchants had many ideas to solve the trash problom: one of the solutions was to put lots of perfume on the trash, another was to cart it out of town, bury it, throw it into the sea and the final solution was to chop it up until you can't see it, touch it or smell it!
>
> The meeting went on for hours but they couldn't find a good solution. It was agreed that they would meet again. Everyone hopes that at the next meeting the will be able to find a solution. All the merchants left holding perfume to their noses!

In contrast, the children wrote mostly three-event narratives (31 percent) when they wrote with their peers (see Table 6.1). Chronology with evaluation was the second most frequently occurring structure (19 percent) in the peer pairs. As shown in the following example, Shara (an African American girl) and Emma (a girl of European descent) reported on several events ("A noble family moved into their new palace," "They had a grat fest") and offered their opinions of these events and aspects of the setting ("biggest palace in florence," "the furniture was pitaful," "picture's made by fameiss artists like michelangelo").

> A noble family moved into their new palace. It was the biggest palace in florence. A hole room was as big as a whale. The furniture was pitaful so they change it. the new furnitrure was the most butiful. They had lots of picture's made by fameiss artists like michelangelo and the building was buld by filoppo brunilescy. after that they had a grat fest. After the feast the gests went outside and looked at the plants and they also saw prity statuses and fuotans.

Chronology with evaluation was also the second most frequent structure in the teacher-student pairs. Peer pairs wrote classic narratives, chronologies, one-event narratives, and miscellaneous or uncategorizable narratives in 13 percent (per category) of the peer collaboration text sample.

Within and across time and children, the narrative structures varied, but given the diversity of cultural and economic backgrounds of the sixteen children in this sample, there was consistency across children in the types of narratives they wrote. A few patterns of change across time, however, emerged and seem to warrant further study. The number of three-event narratives written by children on their own increased from only one at times 1 and 2 to five at time 5 but then decreased to two at times 8 and 9 (for sequence of writing tasks, see Daiute, Campbell, Griffin, Reddy, and Tivnan, this volume, Exhibit 3.1). Many of the children increased from writing fewer to more events over time, evidenced by decreases in one-event narratives in comparison to a variety of other types (most frequently, three-event narratives, but sometimes chronologies, chronologies with evaluation, or classic structures).

When composing individually, the children wrote mostly sequences of events, including two-event narratives (19 percent), three-event narratives (16 percent), and chronologies (14 percent). Fifteen percent of the children's narratives were chronologies with evaluation. Thirteen percent were uncategorizable according to the Peterson and McCabe (1983) schema, but only 8 percent were classic and 3 percent ended at the high point. Thus, the most frequent narrative structures emphasized by the teacher were the least frequent produced individually by the children. The following narrative, written individually by Gary (an African American child), is an example of a two-event narrative because he situates the story in the present and focuses on orientation and evaluation rather than event telling. Gary's here-and-now style was a unique approach to a two-event narrative, so we continue to explore this classification.

> Today Filippo Brunileshey has created the masterpiese of the centery he has done what no man has ever done Filippo has created a dome. right now ther is a croud of more then one million peole orpund his house right now. and more down in the middle of the town where this great masterpeise stands it is decorated with eight arches on each side with a staircaase right up the middle and three balcaneise on each side. We all think this is a great achevment. because the people in charge will make alot of money by charging people alot of money to see this msterpeise. this is Gary sighing off

These results show that the teacher used the collaborative composing sessions to engage children in writing narratives of a form—the classic narrative form as defined by Peterson and McCabe (1983)—that is expected in a school based mostly in white mainstream culture. This form of cultural transmission differs from that of copying models of ideal texts because, in the collaborative context, the child is involved in creating the text with the teacher, especially by contributing content, as we illustrate later. While some educators might consider this teacher's interactions to be too controlling, others might say that she is offering the kind of explicit instruction that children need (Cazden, 1992; Delpit, 1988) in an interactive way that allows them to participate and thus have maximum support for mastering the new forms

(Vygotsky, 1978). Patterns in the children's peer narratives and individual narratives inform these issues of construction and transfer.

The relatively frequent use of classic structure in the teacher-child texts (which were influenced to a great extent by the teacher) indicates that the teacher might have been more focused on the overall structure of the narrative, since the classic form involves coming to closure whereas a chronology with evaluation ends more openly. Thus, the classic form implies that the narrative is shaped around events instead of characters or evaluations of events, as were the narratives the children were more prone to produce, and as narratives in other cultures are more prone to be. Furthermore, the peers' relatively frequent use of the three-event narrative form (31 percent compared to the individuals' use at 16 percent) indicates that together they came closer to the model that the teacher was trying to convey.

The teacher may have been focusing on narrative structure to fulfill her perceived role as a communicator of text values. In fact, when asked to discuss how she thought she would work with the children in the collaborative writing activities, the teacher mentioned tailoring her composing and comments to children's needs, which she considered primarily structural in nature (for example, writing better opening sentences and making their way through a complete story in one sitting, which, as process writing students, they were not accustomed to doing). This choice to be a cultural transmitter is not surprising for a teacher, although this does not mean that she would necessarily take the same approach when writing on her own or with a peer, where structure would be assumed and she could focus relatively more on meaning. Educators have increasingly urged that teachers offer children explicit instruction in culturally privileged discourse forms (Cazden, 1992; Delpit, 1988), yet the issue of which structures are privileged, acceptable, and censored could be considered critically within a literacy curriculum (Friere and Macedo, 1987; Heath and Mangiola, 1991).

When working alone, children wrote mostly two-event narratives, followed in frequency by three-event narratives; thus, individual child authors were not spontaneously using the so-called classic form. This is not surprising given that these were school-related written narratives rather than personal oral narratives. More important, given results of recent research on diverse narrative structures across cultural groups, one might not expect these children in this study, who are from diverse cultural backgrounds, to construct written or oral narratives in classic form. We were, in fact, prepared to formulate new structural descriptions based on the children's written narratives, but the adapted high-point scheme covered over 90 percent of the narratives produced by the sixteen children. The relatively small percentages of narratives in the miscellaneous category (13 percent in collaborative narratives by peers, 13 percent in individually written narratives) indicate that the high-point narrative structure format accounted for most of the data. The miscellaneous category has been expanded during the past ten years to include forms that are typical in other cultures (McCabe, 1992), so, as noted above, we examined these narratives in terms of other organizations as well.

The miscellaneous category was reserved for those narratives whose structures did not clearly match other categories in our modified version of the Peterson and McCabe (1983) narrative schema. Narratives in this category were marked by a focus on evaluation and orientation rather than events. Their structures were less temporally and linearly bound, as narrators of these texts moved in and about their experience of the topics under consideration. The structures of narratives categorized as miscellaneous reflect their authors' responses to the context of the narrative task. Gary, for instance, assumed a television newscaster's stance while narrating, as in the earlier-cited text. Miscellaneous narratives were often written in an engaging manner, with the narrator shaping the text to meet the perceived needs of the audience. These narratives were composed by children from a range of cultural and academic backgrounds.

Evaluation. To gain more detailed information about children's evaluations, we did a separate analysis of types and frequencies of narrative evaluation. Given that the children wrote much shorter narratives when composing with peers and on their own than when composing with their teacher, the children's use of evaluation was relatively dense. Table 6.2 lists the number of evaluations of each type (intensifiers, adjectives, and so on) and overall in texts by teacher-child pairs, peer pairs, and individual children. Since the narratives by children when working with the teacher were considerably longer than the narratives children wrote with peers and individually, we computed the mean number of evaluations per word to illustrate the relative density of evaluation. This computation yields small numbers when these evaluations are broken down by type, but they suggest that children evaluated most overall when writing independently (.18) or with a peer (.16) and least when working with the teacher (.14). While a repeated-measures analysis of variance across these three conditions was not significant ($F[2,30]=1.03, p < .36$), a repeated-measures analysis of variance comparing the mean use of evaluation by children (when writing independently and with a peer) (.17) versus their mean use of evaluation when working with a teacher (.14) did suggest significant differences ($F[1,15]=72.69, p < .0001$). These analyses remain preliminary and will be examined in further in subsequent research, but they do suggest that the children in this context had a penchant for evaluation. These results suggest, then, that even relatively unskilled writers are adept at using written evaluation around academic material to embed opinions.

As shown in Table 6.2, children used a variety of types of evaluation across the different composing conditions. The breakdown by evaluation type shows that children used complex types of evaluation such as qualifying adjectives, causal explanation, and delimiters (*sort of, kind of*), which are more characteristic of oral language. Although the differences in use of intensifiers were not significant across groups, the children used a broad range of

Table 6.2. Mean Frequencies per Word and Evaluations in Texts Written by Teacher-Child Pairs, Peer Pairs, and Individual Children

Evaluation Types	Teacher-Child Texts (N = 32)		Peer Texts (N = 16)		Individual Texts (N = 80)	
	Mean	SD	Mean	SD	Mean	SD
Mean Words per Text	182.70	29.61	69.00	24.53	72.70	34.13
Internal States						
Emotion	1.84	1.76	0.56	0.81	0.44	0.83
Cognition words	2.47	2.72	1.00	1.03	0.89	1.35
Physical state	0.06	0.25	0.00	0.00	0.15	0.46
Intentions	0.91	1.06	0.19	0.40	0.24	0.63
Qualifiers						
Intensifiers	4.00	2.44	2.06	1.91	1.46	1.51
Delimiters	0.88	0.95	0.75	1.18	0.74	1.04
Negation	0.78	1.17	0.44	0.73	0.51	1.03
Qualifying adjectives and adverbs	12.09	5.48	4.19	3.19	3.88	3.49

Linguistic Devices						
Repetition	0.03	0.13	0.00	0.00	0.04	0.17
Onomatopoeia	0.00	0.00	0.00	0.00	0.00	0.00
Simile	0.03	0.13	0.06	0.25	0.03	0.11
Metaphor	0.09	0.30	0.06	0.25	0.01	0.06
Compulsion words	0.34	0.66	0.13	0.34	0.24	0.59
Exaggerations	0.22	0.54	0.06	0.25	0.06	0.29
Fantasy	0.00	0.00	0.00	0.00	0.00	0.00
Emphasis	1.66	2.03	0.75	1.53	3.34	11.04
Causality						
Physical	0.78	1.05	0.69	0.95	0.46	0.76
Psychological	0.25	0.57	0.25	0.45	0.14	0.41
Total Average Evaluations	26.43		11.19			12.63

intensification devices, including many exclamation points, changes in the size of font in the word processor, and upper-case letters. The children's significantly greater use of causal evaluation ($F[2,30] = 7.17, p < .01$) is quite surprising, since explanation is typically considered to be a cognitively more advanced skill. We think that the intense, meaning-based nature of the children's interactions with peers could account for such a difference, and we plan to explore this factor in future research.

The differences in the children's texts when writing with peers and on their own reveal a relatively frequent use of the chronology-with-evaluation form, the second most frequent form used by the peer pairs. In addition to this overall structure of chronology with evaluation, most of the highly frequent one-, two-, and three-event narratives by the children, especially when writing with peers, included extensive evaluation, even though the nature of the event structure did not qualify to identify the overall structure as chronology with evaluation in the Peterson and McCabe (1983) schema.

This relatively frequent use of evaluation among peers suggests, as we hypothesized, that the children used the peer collaboration context for making sense of school material. Working with a peer might feel like a meaningful literacy context because there is an audience, or it might increase one's inclination to evaluate because peers tend to request explanations, clarifications, and other types of engagement around the text. Such intense social interactions might engage children in exploring their interpretations or making commitments to the task that in turn lead children to evaluate. The children's intense evaluation in the texts and their gravitation toward a wide range of meaningful topics in their conversations as they composed may, of course, also have as much to do with a lack of explicit awareness of structural issues as with the need to make sense of the task. Nevertheless, these results indicate that children approach tasks meaningfully and with purpose, as long as their meanings and purposes need not be expressed explicitly or in structural terms. Perhaps because of their naïveté regarding structural expectations for written narrative, they focus on the sense-making functions. This compunction to make sense has been noted repeatedly in the developmental literature (Donaldson, 1978; Piaget, 1967) as well as in research on oral narratives, but when the domain shifts to literacy, structural and surface features often dominate descriptions of children's competence and performance. Researchers and educators need to become more aware of such sense-making strategies by children.

In summary, differences in the types of evaluation in teacher-child and peer-written narrative texts indicate that the teacher guides children in evaluating, mostly through the use of adjectives and adverbs rather than intensifiers. This difference may be one of control over written language, since use of adjectives such as *disgraceful, filthy,* and *pitiful* requires vocabulary knowledge, whereas intensifiers such as *very* and *most* and *-est* comparatives are in relatively frequent oral and written use by the third grade.

Focalization. The focalization analysis offered information about how the authors indicated point of view—in this case, evaluation and narrator's distance from events and characters. This analysis supported our general finding that the children used the narrative context to take control over school material.

The teacher guided her young coauthors in taking external and internal perspectives on the events and characters in their narratives. For example, narratives often began with a story opener that established the setting, characters, and general event, not implying much insider information. Many of the clauses in the teacher-child texts, moreover, included unspecified focus, which is evaluation that occurs from the point of view of some assumed or omniscient narrator rather than from a specific point of view, such as a character's or the author's as explicitly stated in the text. It was slightly more characteristic of the children's collaborative texts to evaluate from a specific point of view, either their own as authors-characters or from the point of view of characters in the texts.

The following three texts by Brant (focalization analysis in square brackets) illustrate how his control over point of view changed over three individual composing sessions.

Task 1
The dayly planet today we are at room 203 at the lh school [internal: author-character focus] *and we will look at thar art* [internal: author-character focus]. *I like evreything* [internal: author-character focus] *but I like the dragin the most* [internal: author-character focus]. *dont you think so* [appeal to reader]

Task 2
fillepoe, brunelesk invented a way to make the dome on santmarry the flwer and the ferst crane in florence [external: author-observer]. *the crane was for lifting hevey rokes that are to hevey for a man to karey* [internal: unspecified focus].

Task 5
MLK SKOOI GO;S TO GARDNER MUSEUM. . . . miss Gardner was loveubewul women [internal: unspecified focus] *she lived on the top of the museum* [external: author-observer] *she played the tackes* [external: author-observer] *her husbend did the woerk* [external: author-observer] *when he died she was left olune all by her self* [internal: character focus] *but she made the best of it . . .* [internal: character focus] *THE END . . . . . . ,*

Brant, like other children, tended more over time to focus narrative events from within the text by removing himself as a character, taking on the role of omniscient narrator and including unspecified evaluation, and, in many cases, expressing evaluation from a character's point of view. As shown in the examples above, Brant is present in the action in task 1 as indicated by his use of *we,* by his expression of his own preferences ("I like the dragin"), and by his direct appeal to his reader ("dont you think so"). Thus, the focalization in this text is internal, and the evaluation is from the author's point of view, although the author shifts from his own point of view to one obviously including his reader. In contrast, Brant pulls away from the events in task 2, with the author observing events, as indicated by the relatively specific contextual information in the first sentence. Finally, in task 5, Brant moves the focus of the narrative to the main character, events in her life, and evaluations that empathize with her point of view.

Although not conclusive in results, the focalization analysis also provides a way of examining and talking about children's connections to their writing by determining relatively external and internal foci and by determining the point of view of evaluation. Examination of children's control over focalization over time reveals diverse patterns across children and suggests a general trend toward increasingly internal focalization, especially after children write with peers. These findings, however, are preliminary and must be examined more extensively in future research. Although the tendency of a child to write more internally focused narratives over time when working on one type of task around a corpus of material might be further documented in subsequent research, we do not think this tendency represents any absolute developmental pattern of focalization. The ability to control and craft one's own stance and interpretation as author and to distinguish these from the points of view of characters in one's texts may increase with maturity. Nevertheless, such control is likely to vary depending on the author's familiarity with a topic.

Finally, focalization analysis is designed to offer insights about how children take control over school content as much as how they take control over the written language genre. The qualitative analyses presented here indicate that children can relate closely to academic material even when it is far from their experience, but they may need specific social and affective contexts like collaborative construction of narratives to support such sense making. Field notes and interviews, in addition to his writing and social interactions around writing, indicate that Brant, for example, was quite struck by the experience of Renaissance art and by Isabella Stewart Gardner as a person and collector of such art, even though one might think that a young, African American boy from a low-income family would not find much interesting about an elderly, rich, white lady who was fascinated with Renaissance Italy. The focalization analysis indicated that Brant, like other children, related closely to a wide range of historical events as well as to personal events. It is, moreover, important to add that the teacher's engaging curriculum allowed the children many types of access to and much control over the material they were studying. Our analysis suggests that the task of writing narratives about these events was one vehicle that supported children's interpretations of, and learning about, times and places far from their actual experience.

Although our sample size is too small to reveal any absolute differences, children's likelihood of using unspecified or character focus did not seem to depend on whether they had worked with a teacher or peer but rather on whether they were collaboratively doing the task. This observation could also be explored in future research.

Narrative Construction Processes. Results of the analysis of narrative script patterns are consistent with this difference in emphasis: on structure by the teacher and on meaning making and affect by the children. The teacher organized her composing sessions with the children around major aspects of narrative structure as emphasized in standard written English. As outlined in Exhibit 6.1 and illustrated in the following dialogue excerpt, the teacher's script when collaborating with children included establishing background content, developing a catchy opening sentence, producing events, establishing a resolution or ending, and rereading the story to check.[1]

Exhibit 6.1. Narrative Script for Teacher-Child and Peer Pairs

Script	
Teacher-Child Pair	*Peer Pair*
Background	What should we write?
Opening sequence	Who writes (types) first, next?
Plot and problem	Event production
Ending, final idea	Character frame
Going back and reading over	Switch places at keyboard
Mention time limit	Reread text

Modules	
Including target vocabulary	Meaning-based topics
Saving computer files	Task elements
Personal sections	Characters (Room 203 kids)
Description	Headline with task topic
	Why event was important

Recurring	
Discuss typing	Discuss procedures
Produce text	Discuss spelling
Review content	Discuss phrasing
Elaborate description	
Orient via questioning	
Mechanics	
Revisions, refinements, corrections	
Structure	

Note: Examples of meaning-based topics are whether Columbus rediscovered America, why Columbus called Indians "Red Indians," why fights occurred among puppeteers, whether Filippo built the walls or just the dome, and the significance of the stolen pictures.

Opening Sequence
TEACHER: Now we need a catcher sentence at the beginning, that's going to get everybody to want to read this story in the newspaper!
GARY: Hmm.

Background
TEACHER: What was significant? What was the most important thing about the printing press? Why was that an important invention?
GARY: It made it easy, it made it easier to copy things, like umm you wouldn't have to write every page or something. Or if you wanted to have copies, you could just put it on the printing press, and it would go easier.
TEACHER: Right. And then people could # could, and then more ideas could spread, because people could write down their ideas and pass it along.

Plot and Problem
TEACHER: And then we can talk about what happened, how Gutenberg wanted to make books beautiful and how this other person wanted to just mass-produce books . . .
GARY: Yeah.
TEACHER: Okay, so # years to write a book. Who did most of the writing before this? Do you remember who did?

Going Back and Reading Over
TEACHER: Someplace else where // where we alread+/ # and that Gutenberg worked for years on this invention, he hoped to make beautiful.
GARY: Yeah, that sounds good.

Description Module (may or may not be present)
TEACHER: Okay. Now why don't you describe about how, what people had to do. Before the print+/ before this great invention what happened before this great invention?
GARY: Um, everybody had, you had to write.
TEACHER: People had to write.
GARY: everything out themselves.
TEACHER: People had # to # write # everything [typing].
GARY: And that was hard because everybody didn't even know how to write.

This script applied to all thirty-two of the transcripts analyzed, with differences only in use of the modules and the specific topics explored over many speaking turns (more than three) in different transcripts. In an interview conducted before the collaborative composing sessions began, the teacher had mentioned these narrative and composing process features as items that her students needed more work on and that she felt would be productively modeled in her collaborations with the children.

A much more general and less structurally specific script emerged from transcripts of the peer composing sessions. The peer pair script, as shown in Exhibit 6.1, included jumping into the task, asking, "What should we write?" rather than prompting for task or background content, and moving along across events, with equal emphasis on characters and events. The peer interactions were punctuated by switching places at the keyboard rather than by narrative or process structures like making sure to come to closure with an ending or resolution or rereading the text to check whether there was anything in need of change. The essence of the peer interactions occurred as each pair happened on topics that they felt compelled to explore in depth.

The following two dialogue excerpts are examples of the meaning-making conversations that characterized peer interactions. In the first example, Andy and Russ deliberate on their imagined landing of Columbus's crew.

ANDY: Discovered!
RUSS: Ya. Discovered Japan! [laughter]
ANDY: Well, no. Discotti. Discovered it. No, we're # fine # Rediscovered then.
RUSS: Okay, rediscovered America # No! It should be New England.
ANDY: Ya, 'cause he did.
RUSS: No, that was in the Revolutionary times.
ANDY: Reduscovered.
RUSS: I wonder if it should be New Spain or New England?
ANDY: Forget it, I mean. Rediscovered America!
RUSS: No, rediscovered the West Indies, thinking it was Japan.
ANDY: Yeah! Yeah! Nice. Alright, we got a smart person here # like moi! [giggle] No, rediscovered. R-E whoa! R-E-S-C, S-C-O, oh, I've got to find the V. I forgot where the V is.

In the second example, Lisa and Kay consider what was important about the class trip.

LISA: Oh, I've got it, I've got it, I've got it!!!!!! At the end, we'll say why it's important, okay? Cuz, remember?
KAY: But how about?
LISA: When we went to the Gardner Museum, the man old+/ who was?
KAY: Yeah.
LISA: The tourist, when he said we # her # someone some # someone rang the doorbell. Th// they heard the door, the doorbell ring and the there were a bunch of police in outfits with gund and stuff, and they were in a disguise, and then they came d— and they and then we would, and then they would said, "We want to take a look at your pictures and tapestries and stuff," and then they took some of those pictures. So remember when we were up on the third floor, and we found, saw all those pictures?
KAY: Yeah.

LISA: And there was a painting here, skip, so painting here, skip.

KAY: Oh, yeh! [Clears throat] And there was bl// there were these places where there's painting used to paintings used to be.

LISA: Yeh, that's those were the ones that were stolen. So that's why we went (?), that's why it was important.

KAY: How 'bout.

LISA: And then they went and sold them so they could get money, like a thousand dollars or something.

KAY: W// well we did. We went to learn about the paintings and everyting, right? Learned everything.

Discussion and Implications

What do the processes and products of written narrative construction among children and their teacher in a third-grade classroom indicate about how children construe school-based literacy tasks? This study offered several insights about the nature of classroom-based writing. Even though paradigms of literacy theory have shifted from an exclusive focus on texts to a focus on literacy processes and context of use, there is still a tendency in research and practice to emphasize structural aspects of texts. For many years, the structural focus supported cognitive categories, for example, of experienced and inexperienced readers and writers. More recently, genre structures reveal cultural categories—children's background discourse styles in contrast to the school's styles. Observations of children working in social contexts with teachers and peers have revealed that while the teacher—like researchers—may emphasize structural features of narratives in the text and in conversations around narrative texts, children use the social context of peer interaction to explore meanings and make sense of school material and school tasks.

The research reported in this chapter explores new methodologies in writing research in relation to the goal of expanding literacy theory. Through our application of methods of oral narrative discourse analysis to written narratives, we have added an affective component to literacy analysis that has been missing from theory and ignored in practice. Examination of how children interpret academic material by using evaluation devices in their writing offers insights about how they empathize with material, characters, and events in their writing, whether it is about the culturally and historically distant Renaissance or an accident in the school. Use of the written narrative as a filter for children's experience with academic material promises to expand our ways of studying and assessing writing.

In addition, this study has shown how peer groups in the third grade can, like the teacher, serve to enculturate children to new discourse forms. While much of the focus of sociocultural analysis has been on family culture, the classroom culture can also play a role in influencing discourse, especially when there is ample room for child-directed discourse, and, we argue, discussion about the diverse nature, functions, and sociopolitical roles of different discourse forms.

The children's talk around narrative constructions with peers tended to be highly social and affectively charged, and the subsequent individual written narratives were elaborated and infused with personal perspectives. In contrast, the teacher-student conversations tended to be cognitive, focusing on narrative categories and literacy topics. While the structural and personal approaches to narrative tend to be relegated to different collaborative composition situations, we find that a balance of the two is the most helpful to children who want eventually to be able to use multiple forms of narrative in and out of school.

As the interactions illustrated in this chapter have shown, the practice of allowing children to take personal, evaluative stances on their classroom material, as they are more likely to do with their peers than with their teacher, intensely involves them in work with a wide range of academic material. Evaluation and empathy are powerful mediators of thought and action for children who do not yet readily use explicit metacognitive skills. Continued examination of relationships between sense making, as we have captured it in our narrative analyses, and children's critical literacy skills may lead to more complex understandings of how people become literate.

Note

1. The following transcript codes are used in this chapter: # = pause, +/ = interrupted speech, // = self-correction, (?) = unclear word or words, . . . = trailing off.

References

Bakhtin, M. M. *Speech Genres and Other Late Essays.* (V. N. McGee, trans.) Austin: University of Texas Press, 1986.

Bal, M. *Narratology.* White Plains, N.Y.: Longman, 1991.

Bamberg, M. "Narrative Activity as Perspective Taking: The Role of Emotionals, Negations, and Voice in the Construction of the Story Realm." *Journal of Cognitive Psychotherapy: An International Quarterly,* 1991, 5, 275–291.

Bransford, J., Vye, N., Adams, L., and Perfetto, G. "Learning Skills and the Acquisition of Knowledge." In A. Lesgold and R. Glaser (eds.), *Foundations for a Psychology of Education.* Hillsdale, N.J.: Erlbaum, 1989.

Bruner, J. *Actual Minds, Possible Worlds.* Cambridge, Mass.: Harvard University Press, 1986.

Cazden, C. *Classroom Discourse: The Language of Teaching and Learning.* Portsmouth, N.H.: Heinemann Educational Books, 1988.

Cazden, C. *Whole Language Plus.* New York: Teachers College Press, 1992.

Daiute, C. "The Role of Play in Writing Development." *Research in the Teaching of English,* 1990, 24, 4–47.

Daiute, C. "Youth Genres: Links Between Sociocultural and Developmental Theories." *Language Arts,* 1993, 70, 62–76.

Daiute, C., and Dalton, B. "Collaboration Between Children Learning to Write: Can Novices Be Masters?" *Cognition and Instruction,* 1993, 10, 1–43.

Delpit, L. D. "The Silenced Dialogue: Power and Pedagogy in Educating Other People's Children." *Harvard Educational Review*, 1988, *58* (3), 280–298.

Donaldson, M. *Children's Minds*. London: Croom Helm, 1978.

Fox, R. "Developing Awareness of Mind Reflected in Children's Narrative Writing." *British Journal of Developmental Psychology*, 1991, *9*, 281–298.

Friere, P., and Macedo, D. *Literacy: Reading the Word and the World*. South Hadley, Mass.: Bergin & Garvey, 1987.

Heath, S. B. *Ways with Words: Language, Life, and Work in Communities and Classrooms*. New York: Cambridge University Press, 1983.

Heath, S. B., and Mangiola, L. *Children of Promise: Literate Activity in Linguistically and Culturally Diverse Classrooms*. Washington, D.C.: National Education Association, 1991.

Hudson, J. A., Gebelt, J., Haviland, J., and Bentivegna, C. "Emotion and Narrative Structure in Young Children's Personal Accounts." *Journal of Narrative and Life History*, 1992, *2*, 129–150.

Hymes, D. H. "Models of the Interactions of Language and Social Life." In J. J. Gumperz and D. H. Hymes (eds.), *Directions in Sociolinguistics: The Ethnography of Communication*. Troy, Mo.: Holt, Rinehart & Winston, 1972.

Labov, W. *Language in the Inner City*. Philadelphia: University of Pennsylvania Press, 1972.

Labov, W., and Waletzky, J. "Narrative Analysis: Oral Versions of Personal Experience." In J. Helm (ed.), *Essays in the Verbal and Visual Arts*. Seattle: American Ethnological Society, 1967.

McCabe, A. "All Kinds of Good Stories." Paper presented at the 42nd annual meeting of the National Reading Conference, San Antonio, Texas, 1992.

McCabe, A., and Peterson, C. (eds.). *Developing Narrative Structure*. Hillsdale, N.J.: Erlbaum, 1991.

Mehan, H. *Learning Lessons: Social Organization in the Classroom*. Cambridge, Mass.: Harvard University Press, 1979.

Michaels, S. "The Dismantling of Narrative." In A. McCabe and C. Peterson (eds.), *Developing Narrative Structure*. Hillsdale, N.J.: Erlbaum, 1991.

Miranda, E., Camp, L., Hemphill, L., and Wolf, D. "Developmental Changes in Children's Use of Tense in Narrative." Paper presented at the annual meeting of the Boston University Conference on Language Development, Boston, Oct. 1992.

Peterson, C., and McCabe, A. *Developmental Psychology: Three Ways of Looking at Children's Narratives*. New York: Plenum, 1983.

Piaget, J. *Six Psychological Studies*. New York: Random House, 1967.

Rodino, A. M., and others. "Contrastive Sequencing in Low-Income African-American and Latino Children's Personal Narratives." Paper presented at the annual meeting of the Boston University Conference on Language Development, Boston, Oct. 1991.

Schank, R., and Abelson, R. *Scripts, Plans, Goals, and Understanding*. Hillsdale, N.J.: Erlbaum, 1977.

Snow, C. E., and Dickinson, D. K. "Social Sources of Narrative Skills at Home and at School." *First Language*, 1990, *10*, 87–103.

Vygotsky, L. S. *Mind in Society: The Development of Higher Psychological Processes*. (M. Cole, V. John-Steiner, S. Scribner, and E. Souberman, eds.) Cambridge, Mass.: Harvard University Press, 1978.

COLETTE DAIUTE *is associate professor at the Graduate School of Education, Harvard University.*

TERRI M. GRIFFIN *is a doctoral candidate in language and literacy at the Graduate School of Education, Harvard University.*

*Although the chapters in this volume differ somewhat in perspective,
focus, and findings, several insights about the nature of literacy emerge
as themes across the chapters.*

Synthesis

Colette Daiute

The contributors to this volume suggest new ways of thinking about literacy,
revealing a complex of issues relating to social interactions around literacy.
In addition to establishing and exploring theoretical foundations, we have
also raised new questions. To synthesize the chapters of this volume, I
present a list of principles that emerge from our research and suggest their
implications for future research and practice. I recognize that more research
on literacy as a social process is required, both for theoretical and practical
purposes.

This synthesis is not the result of a metaanalysis; these principles are hypotheses more than conclusions. Since social orientations to human development and education are promising, and the basic research presented here is
thorough, detailed, and consistent with research across other disciplines,
these principles warrant further exploration.

Children become literate in the context of relationships. Children learn
about the purposes, processes, and forms of written language by working and
playing with text in the context of interactions with parents, teachers, and
peers. This research offers information about characteristics of discourse between parents and children, children and teachers, and among peers that relate to literacy. Interactions with parents and peers introduce affective
orientations to literacy, while teachers appear to stress cognitive and structural categories. There may be predispositions within certain types of relationships that support one or another aspect of literacy, yet, considered
together, these studies suggest that certain types of interactions would support literacy across context. The notion of relationship and the mutual, committed orientations that are possible to explore within relationships are
important.

Literacy is dependent on oral discourse in a variety of ways. The chapters in this volume report, for example, that children who explain, explore, argue, and play with language and ideas—whether with parents, teachers, or peers—are more likely to grow as writers and readers than children who do not use language in these ways. We have found, moreover, that having the chance to engage in such complex processes in their spontaneous oral language styles is especially helpful to children who have begun to fall behind in school-based literacy. One synthesis of these findings is that children also benefit from shifting discourse registers—writing as they would speak and talking in ways that they are expected to write. This volume has identified several specific types of discourse that relate to children's literacy achievement, including reading and writing with peers in their own voices; talking about ideas, objects, processes, and nonpresent events; talking about language; and using spontaneous problem-solving approaches like play to examine language and ideas.

Literacy is a set of social functions, practices, and forms, not a hierarchy of skills based on units of written language. Literacy cannot be defined in terms of mastery of units that build on one another. Rather, children understand the myriad aspects and features of written language as they occur in meaningful contexts, like communication, inquiry, or problem solving. This shift in perspective involves redefining what it means to become literate and what count as basic skills. From this perspective, social discourse is a basic skill.

Beginning literacy users benefit from access to social and emotional as well as cognitive and linguistic resources. Understanding literacy requires perspectives from various disciplines that together can account for children's spontaneous approaches. Several types of interactions revealed children's interpretive approach to school-based tasks. Interpretations revealed through play, narrative evaluation, and explicit expressions of feelings are only some ways that children bring affect into academic tasks, yet such a perspective has not been integrated into theories of literacy development. Previous theory has been successful at explaining expert readers' and writers' approaches, which are quite sophisticated and explicit in the cognitive strategies for literacy, and it would advance theory considerably to be able to reconcile children's strategies, which do not fit neatly into cognitive categories.

Our research, thus, suggests that literacy must be integrated into children's lives, because social and affective interactions support conceptual aspects of academic skills like reading and writing. Additional research is needed to further define an interdisciplinary theory of literacy that integrates social, affective, cognitive, and linguistic aspects of literacy development. In addition, the list of oral discourse functions that relate to written language development could be expanded and explored among different groups of beginning writers and readers across age groups. Research that explores relationships between social, affective, cognitive, and linguistic aspects of literacy and learning should also consider how such explanations relate to instruction—a process that should probably become more social.

Research on literacy should be closely connected to practice. The following suggestions are consistent with the insights listed above but are phrased to emphasize implementation and exploration in classroom contexts.

Although our understanding of literacy as a social process reveals the central role of discourse in reading and writing development, existing curricula do not support that foundation. The strong social grounding of literacy discussed by Dyson; the important discourse functions identified by Snow and Dickinson, Cote, and Smith; and the importance of children's control over the curriculum demonstrated in the work by Daiute, Campbell, Griffin, Reddy, and Tivnan suggest a shift away from curriculum design that includes lists of skills and a move toward understanding more about the nature of the social contexts that could help children most in the classroom. This research also suggests a need for multiple contexts, with social functions, challenging inquiries, and children's voices as the organizing principles. Discourse, rather than skills, would be at the center of such a curriculum. Projects in this context should involve literacy that serves children's social, emotional, and intellectual purposes and should increase children's awareness of their discourse practices and choices.

This context should include various kinds of diversity, including more opportunities to work with written language in the context of diverse relationships. Children can benefit from collaborating with an expert who reveals his or her expert strategies, but children also need to be allowed to work as experts with peers.

Since discourse genres evolve in sociocultural contexts, children should have experiences with a variety of oral and written genres to serve a variety of purposes, and they should be involved in explicit discussions of the nature, choices, and consequences of such genres, including oral and written genres that are not typically dealt with in school.

To invite children's interpretations of content, events, and people in school, we need to avoid an emphasis on structure. Although highlighting the structures underlying diverse genres would sometimes be useful, the meaning base of education needs to be established from diverse perspectives, which students as well as teachers can introduce. This point relates to the complex nature of literacy and learning and the need to allow children to interpret the contents and processes of education.

Another way of addressing the issue of students' control over their literacy and learning is to ensure that they have sufficient time to work with written language in their own terms. The process of meaning-making is, as we have shown in the various excerpts in this volume, an effortful one, often requiring many utterances for exploration, detours, and discovery. Socially, emotionally, and intellectually meaningful projects can contribute to allowing children control over the curriculum. In addition, peer collaboration and an openness to a range of problem-solving strategies can be helpful.

Many of these approaches have been mentioned by other researchers and educators. The focus of this volume is the social foundation of discourse, the complexity of human discourse, and the interrelatedness of children's lives, literacy, and learning. Focusing on literacy in the social sphere highlights the importance of multiple, complex voices.

COLETTE DAIUTE *is associate professor at the Graduate School of Education, Harvard University.*

INDEX

Abelson, R., 100
Activities, 43, 45; writing, 1–2, 50–52
Adams, L., 100
Affective talk style, 56
Ahrens, M., 20
Allen, J., 71
Alsalam, N., 75
Ambrose, R. P., 92
Analysis of variance (ANOVA), 49, 109
Anderson, R., C., 15, 67, 68, 69, 70
Applebee, A. W., 50, 89
Arnold, D. S., 17

Bakhtin, M. M., 2, 35, 99, 101
Bal, M., 104
Bamberg, M., 104
Barone, D., 92
Barringer, F., 75
Beals, D., 20, 22, 68
Beck, I. L., 68
Beers, J. W., 80, 81
Bell, A., 84
Bentivegna, C., 99
Bereiter, C., 43, 61
Blazer, B., 80
Block, K. K., 90
Blum-Kulka, S., 19
Books. See Reading
Bouffler, C., 82
Bransford, J., 100
Broad range focus, 54
Brown, A., 43
Brown, J. S., 42, 45, 61
Bruneau, B. J., 92
Brunelleschi, F., 85, 102
Bruner, J., 26, 99
Buchanan, E., 81

Camp, L., 102, 103
Campbell, C. H., 30, 82, 102, 107
Cancino, H., 18, 68, 72
Carey, S., 70
Cazden, C. B., 17, 35, 92, 100, 101, 107, 108
Chafe, W., 49
Chall, J. S., 79
CHILDES language analysis system, 49, 72

Chomsky, C., 81
Classic structure, 58, 103, 105, 107–108
Clay, M. M., 26, 92
Collaboration: effect of, on writing, 57–60, 105, 106–118; expert, 42–43; peer, 43–45, 88–90, 106–119; social interaction during, 55–57; teacher, 42–43, 90–92, 105, 106–118. See also Communication
Collins, A., 42, 45, 61
Columbus, C., 44, 87, 97
Communication, 1, 122–123. See also Collaboration
Content focus, 52, 53
Context: cultural, 25–26, 99–100; and learning words, 69–71
Context focus, 54
Conversations, adult-child, 71
Cordeiro, P., 80
Corson, D., 75
Cote, L., 12, 15, 21
Cultural context: and literacy, 25–26; and storytelling, 99–100

Daiute, C., 30, 42, 45, 49, 50, 52, 55, 59, 80, 82, 86, 99, 102, 107
Dale-Chall list, 72
Dalton, B., 42, 45, 50, 59, 80, 102
D'Amato, J. D., 34
Danielewicz, J., 49
Davidson, R., 19
Decontextualized language, 36–37, 68–69
Deficits, in child, 1
Defining words, as language skill, 17–18, 22
Delpit, L. D., 101, 107, 108
Desberg, P., 84
DeTemple, J. M., 18, 22, 68, 74
DeVilliers, P. A., 70
Dickinson, D. K., 12, 15, 21, 22, 68, 69, 70, 71, 72, 74, 75, 100
Direct feedback style, 56
Discourse, 1, 122–123. See also Collaboration
DiStephano, J., 84
Diverse media, 28
Donaldson, M., 112

Downing, J., 84
Drum, P. A., 69, 70
Dunn, J., 34
Dyson, A. H., 28, 30, 35, 79, 80

Ehri, L. C., 81
Elaborated classic narrative structure, 58
Empathy, 98, 114, 119
Encoding, 79, 80
Environmental interaction, 2–3, 26, 28
Ervin-Tripp, S., 30
Evaluation, 103–104, 109–112, 119
Expertise, 42–43

Fairbanks, M. M., 68
Family interaction: and definitions, 22; and literacy, 11–12; and storytelling/describing pictures, 21–22, 99; and vocabulary, 20–21, 71
Feitelson, D., 71
Ferdman, B., 34
Ferriero, E., 3
Flower, L., 61
Fluent/decentered structure, 58
Focalization, 104, 113–115
Form and function of symbols, 30–34
Fox, R., 100
Freebody, P., 15, 67, 68
Friedman, M., 84
Friere, P., 108

Gamoran, A., 42
Gardner, I. S., 114
Gebelt, J., 99
Gee, J., 2
Genres, language, 2, 34, 35, 99–100, 123
Gentry, J. R., 81
Gillet, J. W., 81
Goldfield, B. A., 71
Goldstein, Z., 71
Golomb, C., 29
Gonzalez, P., 68, 72
Goodman, K., 79, 81
Grammar: after collaboration, 57–58; as language skill, 16, 17
Graves, D. H., 37, 46, 81, 83
Graves, M. F., 68, 69
Gray, B., 37
Greene, S., 42
Griffin, T. M., 30, 50, 55, 82, 102, 107
Guidance, 42–43

Hartup, W. W., 30
Haste, H., 26
Haviland, J., 99
Hayes, D., 20
Hayes, J., 61
Heath, S. B., 34, 35, 99, 108
Hemphill, L., 102, 103
Henderson, E. H., 81
Herman, P. A., 68, 69, 70
Hirschler, J. M., 74
Hoban, R., 14
Home-School Study of Language and Literacy Development, 21, 22, 68, 71–75
Hudson, J. A., 99
Hughes, M., 30
Hymes, D. H., 104

Information, and language, 36
Intense engagement style, 56
Interpretation, and narratives, 97–99
Iraqi, J., 71

Jenkins, J. R., 69, 70
Jenkins, L., 50
Juel, C., 13

Karweit, N., 71
King, M. L., Jr., 25–26
Kita, B., 71
Konopak, B. C., 69, 70
Kurland, B., 21, 22

LaBerge, D., 79
Labov, W., 99, 102
Langer, J. A., 50, 89
Language: decontextualized, 36–37, 68–69; genres, 2, 34, 35, 99–100, 123; oral and written, 6, 15, 18, 97, 123. See also Oral language; Written language
Letter recognition, 13
Levin, J. R., 68
Literacy development: and cognitive processes, 1; defined, 12, 122; and expertise, 42–43; and family interaction, 1–2, 11–12, 20–23, 71; model, 12–20; and peer interaction, 1–2, 28–30, 43–45; research, 1–2, 6–7, 122–124; and social context, 1–2, 3, 121, 122; and symbols, 25–26; and teacher interaction, 1–2, 42–43, 50–54, 71; and written narratives, 100, 118–119

McCabe, A., 71, 99, 102, 103, 105, 107, 109, 112
McCartney, K., 71
McDaniel, M. A., 68
Macedo, D., 108
McGee, L. M., 81
McKeown, M. G., 68
MacWhinney, B., 49
Mangiola, L., 108
Mapping, 73
Markman, E. M., 70
Marsh, G., 84
Mason, J. M., 71
Mediated action, 28, 31
Mehan, H., 100
Methodology, 7
Mezynski, K., 68
Michaels, S., 17, 100, 101
Middleton, D., 43
Miranda, E., 102, 103
Morris, D., 92
Morson, G. S., 34
Mullis, I. V., 50, 89

Nagy, W. E., 68, 69, 70
Narrative focus, 54
Narratives: analyses of composing of, 104–105; analyses of text of, 102–104; construction of, 104–105, 115–118; evaluation in, 103–104, 109–112; focalization analysis of, 104, 113–115; interpretive functions of, 97–99, 112; and literacy research, 100, 102; oral, 99–100; structure of, 103, 105–109
Narrative/strategy focus, 52–53
Newman, S., 42, 45, 61
Nystrand, M., 42

Ochs, E., 34
Ogle, L. T., 75
Olson, D., 36
Omanson, R. C., 68
Oral language: and family interaction, 1, 12, 20–23; interpretive functions of, 97, 98, 99–100; skills, 15–18; and teaching/explaining information, 36; and written language, 6, 15, 18. See also Language; Talk

Palincsar, A., 43
Parents. See Family interaction

Peabody Picture Vocabular Test (PPVT), 21, 72 73
Pearson, P. D., 69, 70
Peer interaction: and collaboration, 43–45, 88–90, 106–119; effect of, on writing, 58, 59–60; and evaluation, 109–112; and focalization, 114–115; and literacy talk, 50–52; and narrative construction, 115, 117–118; and narrative structure, 106–108; role of, 28–30; and spelling talk, 86–88; styles, 55–57, 61; talk patterns in, 54–55; through talk/activity, 43–45; and vocabulary, 73
Perfetto, G., 100
Performances, 35–36
Personalized narrative focus, 54
Peskowitz, N. B., 90–91
Peterson, C., 99, 102, 103, 105, 107, 109, 112
Phoneme mapping, 13
Phoneme segmentation, 13
Piaget, J., 2, 112
Picture descriptions, as language skill, 15–17, 21–22
Play, 61, 87–88, 121
Pomerantz, S. B., 70
Pressley, M., 68
Principal components analysis (PCA), 49
Problem spaces, 12–13, 18–20
Production, and spelling talk, 83–84
Pronuncation, as language skill, 15
Putnam, L., 71

Radebaugh, M. R., 92
Rasinski, T. V., 92
Read, C., 26, 81
Reading: books, 11, 70–71, 73–75; college-level, ability, 12–13; comprehension, 14–15, 67–68; in family, 11, 23; and oral language skills, 15, 18; performance, 1; skills, 13–15; and spelling, 80; and vocabulary, 70–71, 73–75. See also Written language
Reddy, M., 30, 82, 102, 107
Research, literacy, 1–2, 6–7, 122–124
Responsive teacher style, 56
Rice, M. L., 69, 70
Rich, G., 84
Richgels, D. J., 81
Rodino, A. M., 99

Rogers, G. T., 75
Rogoff, B., 42

Sachs, J., 70
Samuels, S. J., 79
Scaffolding, 43
Scardamalia, M., 43, 61
Schank, R., 100
Schema theory, 100
Schickedanz, J. A., 92
Schlagal, R. C., 81, 88
Schley, S., 18
Scibior, O., 80, 84
Seda, M., 92
Self-monitoring, as language skill, 17
Self-repair mechanisms, 17, 18
Sense-making function, 97-99, 112
Share, D. L., 71
Shaughnessy, M. P., 80
Shriberg, E., 68, 72
Smith, C. A., 70
Smith, M. W., 12, 15, 21, 69, 72, 74
Smith, T. M., 75
Smitherman, G., 35
Snow, C. E., 11, 12, 18, 19, 21, 22, 49, 50,
    68, 69, 71, 100
Social class comparisons, 11
Social cohesion, 35
Social context, and literacy, 1-2, 3, 121,
    122
Social interaction: vs. environmental in-
    teraction, 2-3, 26, 28; and literacy, 1-
    2, 3, 42-45, 121-122; and oral lan-
    guage skills, 1, 12, 20-23; perspectives
    on, 5-6; and symbols, 25-26. See also
    Family interaction; Peer interaction;
    Teacher interaction
Social thought, 2
Speech genres, 2, 34, 35, 99-100, 123.
    See also Talk
Spelling: episode, 85; and memory, 92;
    and peer collaboration, 88-90; re-
    search, 81-82, 93; stages, 81-82; strat-
    egies, 82; study data, 82-84; talk, 84-
    88; and teacher collaboration, 90-92;
    and writing, 79-80
Stahl, S., 68
Stanovitch, K., 13
Stein, M. L., 69, 70
Sternberg, R. J., 69, 70
Storytelling: and cultural context, 99-

100; as language skill, 15, 17, 21-22.
    See also Narratives
Structure focus, 52, 53
Subjectivity, of narratives, 99
Sulzby, E., 71
Symbols: and diverse media, 28; form and
    function of, 30-34; and literacy, 25-26;
    and peer interaction, 28-30; situated
    nature of, 34-37; and social vs. envi-
    ronmental focus, 26, 28

Tabors, P., 17, 20, 21
Talk: collaborative, 43-44; patterns, 52-
    55, 74; social structure, 55-57; spelling,
    84-88; and writing, 60. See also
    Storytelling
Tannen, D., 35
Teacher control style, 56
Teacher interaction: and collaboration,
    42-43, 90-92, 105, 106-118; effect of,
    on writing, 58-60; and evaluation,
    109-112; and focalization, 113-115;
    and literacy talk, 50-52; and narrative
    construction, 115-116; and narrative
    structure, 105, 106-108; and spelling
    talk, 86; styles, 55-57, 61; talk patterns
    in, 52-54, 74; and vocabulary, 71, 73-
    74
Teale, W., 71
Teberosky, A., 2
Templeton, S., 81, 84
Tenney, Y. J., 84, 91
Text form focus, 52, 53
Tivnan, T., 30, 82, 102, 107
Tizard, B., 30
Toward classic structure, 58

United National International School
    study, 22

Valdez-Menchaca, M. C., 71
Velasco, P., 22
Venezky, R. L., 22
Vocabulary: context and, growth, 69-71;
    and family interaction, 20-21, 71; and
    Home-School Study of Language and
    Literacy Development, 68, 71-75; and
    language skill, 15, 68-69; and peer in-
    teraction, 73; and reading books, 70-
    71, 73-75; and reading comprehen-
    sion, 67-68; and teacher interaction,

71, 73–74; and world knowledge, 15, 68, 69
Vye, N., 100
Vygotsky, L. S., 2, 25, 28, 42, 43, 79, 108

Wachtel, G. F., 70
Waletzky, J., 99, 102
Watson, R., 22, 72
Welch, V., 84
Wells, G., 68
Wertsch, J. V., 28
Whitehurst, G. J., 71
Wide range style, 56
Wiemelt, J., 42
Wilde, S., 80, 82, 84, 92
Wixson, K. K., 69
Wolf, D., 102, 103
Wood, D., 43
Woodsmall, L., 70
Words: learning, 69–71; rare, 20–21, 72–

73; recognition of, 13–14; *See also* Spelling; Vocabulary
World knowledge, 15, 68, 69
Writing: activities, 1–2, 50–52; effect of collaboration on, 57–60; interpretive functions of, 97–99; performance, 1; and spelling, 79–80; and talk, 60. *See also* Narratives; Written language
Written language: decontextualized, 35–37; and family interaction, 1, 12; interpretive functions of, 97–99; as mediated action, 28, 31; and oral languaged, 6, 15, 18; situated nature of, 37. *See also* Language; Reading; Writing
Wysocki, K., 69, 70

Zajac, R., 50
Zone of proximal development, 42
Zutell, J., 80

ORDERING INFORMATION

NEW DIRECTIONS FOR CHILD DEVELOPMENT is a series of paperback books that presents the latest research findings on all aspects of children's psychological development, including their cognitive, social, moral, and emotional growth. Books in the series are published quarterly in Fall, Winter, Spring, and Summer and are available for purchase by subscription and individually.

SUBSCRIPTIONS for 1993 cost $54.00 for individuals (a savings of 25 percent over single-copy prices) and $75.00 for institutions, agencies, and libraries. Please do not send institutional checks for personal subscriptions. Standing orders are accepted.

SINGLE COPIES cost $17.95 when payment accompanies order. (California, New Jersey, New York, and Washington, D.C., residents please include appropriate sales tax.) Billed orders will be charged postage and handling.

DISCOUNTS for quantity orders are available. Please write to the address below for information.

ALL ORDERS must include either the name of an individual or an official purchase order number. Please submit your order as follows:
  Subscriptions: specify series and year subscription is to begin
  Single copies: include individual title code (such as CD59)

MAIL ALL ORDERS TO:
  Jossey-Bass Publishers
  350 Sansome Street
  San Francisco, California 94104-1310

FOR SINGLE-COPY SALES OUTSIDE OF THE UNITED STATES CONTACT:
  Maxwell MacMillan International Publishing Group
  866 Third Avenue
  New York, New York 10022-6221

FOR SUBSCRIPTION SALES OUTSIDE OF THE UNITED STATES, contact any international subscription agency or Jossey-Bass directly.

OTHER TITLES AVAILABLE IN THE
NEW DIRECTIONS FOR CHILD DEVELOPMENT SERIES
William Damon, Editor-in-Chief

CD60   Close Friendships in Adolescence, *Brett Laursen*
CD59   The Role of Play in the Development of Thought, *Marc H. Bornstein,*
        Anne Watson O'Reilly
CD58   Interpretive Approaches to Children's Socialization, *William A. Corsaro,*
        Peggy J. Miller
CD57   Beyond the Parent: The Role of Other Adults in Children's Lives
        Robert C. Pianta
CD56   The Development of Political Understanding: A New Perspective,
        Helen Haste, Judith Torney-Purta
CD55   Emotion and Its Regulation in Early Development, *Nancy Eisenberg,*
        Richard A. Fabes
CD54   Narrative and Storytelling: Implications for Understanding Moral
        Development, *Mark B. Tappan, Martin J. Packer*
CD53   Academic Instruction in Early Childhood: Challenge or Pressure?
        Leslie Rescorla, Marion C. Hyson, Kathy Hirsh-Pasek
CD52   Religious Development in Childhood and Adolescence, *Fritz K. Oser,*
        W. George Scarlett
CD51   Shared Views in the Family During Adolescence, *Roberta L. Paikoff*
CD50   Adolescents in the AIDS Epidemic, *William Gardner, Susan G. Millstein,*
        Brian L. Wilcox
CD49   Child Care and Maternal Employment: A Social Ecology Approach,
        Kathleen McCartney
CD48   Children's Perspectives on the Family, *Inge Bretherton, Malcolm W. Watson*
CD47   The Legacy of Lawrence Kohlberg, *Dawn Schrader*
CD46   Economic Stress: Effects on Family Life and Child Development,
        Vonnie C. McLoyd, Constance A. Flanagan
CD45   Infant Stress and Coping, *Michael Lewis, John Worobey*
CD42   Black Children and Poverty: A Developmental Perspective, *Diana T. Slaughter*
CD40   Parental Behavior in Diverse Societies, *Robert A. LeVine,*
        Patrice M. Miller, Mary Maxwell West
CD39   Developmental Psychopathology and Its Treatment, *Ellen D. Nannis,*
        Philip A. Cowan
CD37   Adolescent Social Behavior and Health, *Charles E. Irwin, Jr.*
CD36   Symbolic Development in Atypical Children, *Dante Cicchetti, Marjorie Beeghly*
CD35   How Children and Adolescents View the World of Work, *John H. Lewko*
CD31   Temperament and Social Interaction in Infants and Children,
        Jacqueline V. Lerner, Richard M. Lerner
CD24   Children in Families Under Stress, *Anna-Beth Doyle, Dolores Gold,*
        Debbie S. Moscowitz
CD22   Adolescent Development in the Family, *Harold D. Grotevant, Catherine R. Cooper*
CD19   Children and Divorce, *Lawrence A. Kurdek*